Bringing
Home the
Business

Bringing Home the Business

The 30 Truths Every
Home Business Owner
Must Know

Kim T. Gordon

A Perigee Book

A Perigee Book
Published by The Berkley Publishing Group
A division of Penguin Putnam Inc.
375 Hudson Street
New York, New York 10014

First edition: March 2000

Published simultaneously in Canada.

The Penguin Putnam Inc. World Wide Web site address is
http://www.penguinputnam.com

Library of Congress Cataloging-in-Publication Data

Gordon, Kim T.
Bringing home the business : the 30 truths every home
business owner must know /
Kim T. Gordon.
p.   cm.
Includes index.
ISBN0-399-52598-X
1. Home-based businesses—Management.   2. Customer relations.
3. Marketing.   4. Success in business.
I. Title.
HD62.38.G67   2000
658'.041—dc21   99-056207
CIP

Printed in the United States of America

10   9   8   7   6   5   4   3   2   1

This book is dedicated to all the home business owners who wake up every morning to a greater enjoyment of their lives and work, and to my husband, Stephen Mizner, who helps make it possible for me to do the same.

CONTENTS

CONTENTS

CONTENTS

INTRODUCTION

By reading just one "truth" per day, in thirty days you'll master a complete course on home business success.

■ ■ ■

Every good relationship is based on the truth. Yet for many of us, truth is hard to come by. Particularly when it comes to one subject jam-packed with misconceptions—the home-based business.

Did you know that one-third of all Americans do some or all of their work from home, and at least 24 million own their own home-based businesses? Whether you're planning to start a home-based business or have run one for years, the single most important element you need is *customers or clients*. And that's what *Bringing Home the Business* is about—winning and keeping customers—plus important guidance on living and working successfully under the same roof.

Each chapter presents one of thirty "truths"—vital concepts that, once learned, will have a dramatic impact on your bottom line. These straightforward truths about successfully marketing your home business are combined with expert, step-by-step information to increase your income and create the lifestyle you've always wanted. At the end of each chapter is a checklist of steps that summarize the information so you can immediately put it to work. *Bringing Home the Business* will be especially helpful to busy home business owners for whom *time* is a chief concern. You can read one "truth" each day, and in less than a month you'll have the information you need to start your own business or increase your chances for home business success.

Home-based business owners tend to approach working from home in one of two ways. There are those who view their home offices as a place to start. Apple Computer, for example, is just one of countless companies that are now household names that began as a home-based business. But for the majority of new home business owners, choosing to live and work under the same roof is a lifestyle decision. They want to achieve business success in order to increase their personal incomes. So it's not surprising that home business owners have significantly higher household incomes (approximately sixty thousand dollars a year) than the average American worker, and a sizable percentage have earnings in the six-figure range. *Bringing Home the Business* will be a valuable guide whether your goal is to someday run a Fortune 500 company, or you're looking for a steady increase in business in order to achieve the lifestyle you and your family desire.

The truth is, the move toward working from home is a trend, not a fad. The numbers will increase as larger businesses continue to downsize, and as more and more men and women seek meaningful lifestyles. Americans' values have changed and so has our vision of success. Since the mid nineties, studies have documented the dramatic transformation in Americans' attitudes toward work and success. Now, both men and women are more likely to define success as:

- Having a happy family life or relationship

- Having enough time for family and friends

- Being in control of their lives

Not surprisingly, these are the principal benefits of owning your own home-based business.

Over twenty years' experience in marketing, along with my total commitment to speaking, writing, and consulting on home office success since the late eighties, gives me a unique and comprehensive perspective on the subject. Every year, I have the opportunity to meet thousands of home business owners one-on-one, and many of their stories are in this book.

All of them, in their own fashion, are searching for the best way to market their home-based businesses and increase their success. They tell me they want simple, easy-to-find solutions. They don't want to spend the time or money to study marketing or read small business marketing books written for companies with bigger budgets and support staff to do the grunt work. They want information tailored specifically to their needs that's easy to follow and proven to work. *Bringing Home the Business* has been created for all the home business owners who simply cannot find the answers they're searching for anywhere else. It's the first book written exclusively for those who want to run a successful home-based business that's designed to separate the fact from fiction, debunk all the misconceptions that can lead to business failure, and provide the truths to save you from them.

Bringing Home the Business differs significantly from other home business books. You'll find it contains in-depth information, plus specific recommendations and resources, on a wider range of topics than you'll find elsewhere. It's filled with stories of successful home business owners in a fascinating range of fields nationwide. And it's up to date on new tools and software, plus Internet marketing strategies—from electronic newsletters to associate programs for building income on your Web site.

Read a truth per day, and just one month from now you'll know how to:

- Position your business and create a high-quality image.

- Select a unique niche market.

- Focus your efforts on your most qualified prospects.

- Develop prospect lists, build leads, and write terrific sales letters.

- Find time-saving tools and software to streamline your work.

- Choose the right strategies and budget for your marketing program.

- Create sales and marketing tools that motivate prospects.

- Uncover objections and close more sales.

- Safely buy advertising and select direct mail lists.

- Adopt PR tactics that get you noticed.

- Polish your public speaking skills.

- Set up a program to win referrals.

- Use the Internet to market your business nationally and internationally.

- Adopt strategies that increase customer satisfaction.

- Positively involve family in your business.

- Establish strong personal boundaries and work habits.

- Use strategic partnerships to build your business.

- Combat isolation and work effectively in (and out) of your home office.

- Live and work successfully under the same roof.

Are you ready to increase your business success? Do you want to be in control of your own life and work? Then read on.

ONE

Motivate Your Customers

Truth: To motivate prospects and customers, you must answer their question, "What's in it for me?"

■ ■ ■

The most fundamental truth, and the one that will have the greatest impact on your business success, is this: There's an enormous difference between what you're selling and what your customers or clients are buying. Chances are, you think you're selling your product, your service, your company, or even yourself. But your customers are buying what they are going to receive when they use your product or service. When it comes to communicating with prospects and customers, this is the bottom line: It's not about what you have to offer. Instead, it's all about what the customers or clients will get. Before you can successfully build your business, you must understand this basic principle.

Here's an example. If you were a major potato chip manufacturer, you might have done research with the potato chip–eating public all around the country to determine what they wanted in a new potato chip. And let's say you found out they wanted potato chips that were made without preservatives and came in a resealable bag. That's not what you'd market. You'd market what the potato chip–eating public would gain by these advantages, or features, of your new potato chip. Because they come in a resealable bag, they'll stay fresher longer, and since they're made without preservatives, they may be healthier for you. So, the potato chip manufacturer would market *the fresher, good-for-you potato chip.*

No matter what product or service your company offers, you'll sell more of it and grow your home business steadily over time if you adopt this communications strategy.

FEATURES AND BENEFITS

Features are the characteristics of your product or service and of your company itself. *Benefits* are what motivate prospects to buy. No ad, no brochure, no direct mail piece or face-to-face sales presentation can succeed unless it speaks directly to the benefits your prospects will derive and answers their most prominent question, "What's in it for me?"

Characteristics such as price, location, awards won, length of time in business, size of business, product description, service offering, customer service policies, billing and payment procedures, and so on are all features. If you're a CPA with fifteen years' experience, that experience is a feature. It won't motivate anyone to select you until you translate that feature into a benefit to which your target audience, your prospects, can easily relate. For example, with fifteen years' experience, it's likely you will know the tax codes, make fewer mistakes, and understand opportunities for reducing clients' tax burdens. So the bottom-line benefit to clients of your fifteen years' experience is that you'll help them *save money on their taxes.*

■ Develop a Benefit Statement

To make sure all your written materials and verbal interactions motivate prospects, always put the benefits front and center. Quite possibly, the most important thing you could do today would be to develop a single, unified benefit statement, which will become the crux of your sales and marketing message. It will be the platform from which all the copy for your brochures and ads are developed. Even your voicemail message and the introduction you use when networking will be based on this single statement.

List Features. The best way to develop your own unique benefit statement is to begin by making a comprehensive list of all the features (characteristics) of your company, its products, or services. Don't be surprised if you have a list of at least twenty-five features. Even if you're just starting your home-based business, you can draw on your past experience to flesh out the list.

Let's say you're a mechanical engineer, and you've just invented a piece of equipment that will revolutionize the way a particular manufacturing process is performed worldwide. (Good for you!) You've just started your business and you're developing a benefit statement that will be the basis for the key selling messages in your marketing tools and materials. You'd begin by listing all the principal features of your new piece of equipment, including that it has only eight moving parts instead of sixteen, it incorporates digital computer technology, and it takes up less than three feet of floor space. It's also easy to install and comes with on-site training.

Next, you'd list the special characteristics of your new company itself, including features such as free ongoing technical support and delivery guaranteed in five days or less to anywhere in the United States. Your background in mechanical engineering and experience prior to founding your firm would also be important features, so your list would include your experience in the field, past inventions or successes, and any awards you'd won.

Like this mechanical engineer and his fictitious product, your own business is uniquely yours and unlike any other. So features that pertain to your skills, background, and attitudes toward customers or clients should not be overlooked.

List Benefits. When your comprehensive list of features is complete, you're ready to translate them into a much shorter list of benefits. It's shorter because groups of features, often as many as six or eight, will all translate into the same benefit. And benefits always answer the question from the prospect's point of view, "What's in it for me?"

So if you've invented a machine with only eight moving parts (not sixteen like the older model), that's an important feature. To translate it into a benefit, consider all the ramifications once that product is on the factory floor. With only eight moving parts, there's less opportunity for something to go wrong, which means there will be fewer breakdowns. Purchasers can expect fewer hours or days lost while costly repairs are being made. So your new product reduces downtime, increases efficiency, and (here's the real bottom line) "helps customers increase production" thanks to less downtime. You can take this example a step further and consider what's in it for customers if they increase production. *Increased profitability or sales*, of course.

Intangible versus Tangible Benefits. Benefits may be "intangible" as well as "tangible," like the ones above. Consider this: What's the difference between buying a Chevrolet, an Oldsmobile, or a BMW? Presumably, all three will get you from point A to point B. But when you park that BMW or any other luxury car in your driveway, it confers a certain level of status—an intangible, yet very important benefit to many luxury car buyers.

Here's another example. Let's say you're selling a computer system to a midlevel manager in a major corporation. And let's suppose your system is put in place in several divisions within the corporation, where it performs superbly. Departmental training goes well, the system is user-friendly and requires little maintenance, and the entire project comes in on budget. What are the benefits you have provided to that middle manager? Yes, he has achieved all the benefits previously mentioned, but what's really in it for him?

To understand the answer, you have to consider intangible benefits. Thanks to his decision to purchase your system, which is performing well, was delivered on budget, and helps the corporate divisions function in a superior manner, he will look good to his own superiors. Perhaps he'll get a raise, expand his own department, add staff, and increase his power within the organization. In other words, the middle manager will enhance his own position thanks to the performance of your company. As you can see, intangible benefits often include things like peace of mind and enhanced status and position.

Writing a Benefit Statement. Once you have a list of four to six benefits, you can then create the benefit statement. This is accomplished by stringing a short list of key benefits together into an outer-directed sentence that begins with the name of your company. For example, "Jones and Clarke CPAs will help you save money on corporate taxes, improve your cash flow, and enjoy the peace of mind that comes from having a knowledgeable, highly experienced accounting service behind you." The phrases "save money," "improve your cash flow," and "enjoy peace of mind" are the three principal benefits. The rest of the sentence that follows uses features to expand upon (or explain) the benefits: ". . . that comes from having a knowledgeable, highly experienced accounting service behind you."

▪ The Benefits of a Home-Based Business

In 1988, I was a senior executive with a multibillion-dollar corporation. When I departed to found my own consulting practice, I decided to use a large family room space in my home. I viewed it as a tranquil oasis after the high-stress environment where I was available on demand to the other members of the executive committee and senior managers, the heads of our sixty-two offices and their thirty-eight hundred sales associates, plus my own direct staff. This would be a quiet, productive haven where I could build the kind of company I had envisioned for years. But when I based my private practice in my home, I was unprepared for the reaction I got from the press and colleagues. They clearly perceived my home office situation as a drop in status. The public perception of a home business was that it wasn't real—that I was creating a job for myself and nothing more.

Since then, the perception of home-based businesses has taken a 180-degree turn, and those who have hired home-based business owners and used their products or services now realize the significant benefits of doing so.

Home-based businesses have lower overheads than other small businesses, which must pay a thousand dollars or more per month for the same amount of space. This can mean lower costs to the customer in the long run. Studies show home-based business owners tend to have ten to twenty years' experience before founding their companies. So when clients or customers choose to work with a home-based business owner, they often interact directly with a person who has significant expertise in their field. And there's something to be said for working directly with the boss. Even when home-based business owners team or partner to fulfill contracts, they generally do so with other equally expert individuals. On the other hand, when clients or customers hire a non-home-based business to do the same job, they generally find themselves working with junior-level employees with significantly less experience and know-how.

So here we are at the turn of the century, and 24 million people own their own home-based businesses. With millions more starting each year, you're most likely to be envied by your friends and colleagues when you tell them you work from home. The truth is, it's just too hard to overlook the benefits of owning a home-based business and even harder to ignore the benefits of hiring one. The first year I worked from home in my own business, I earned more money than I ever did working in a corporate corner office. And that's because once clients understood the benefits of hiring my firm, they simply didn't care *where* my desk was located.

Starting today, use benefits to begin every sales and marketing transaction. Explain your benefits with features—never the other way around—just like in the potato chip example: "These new potato chips are good for you and stay fresher longer because they're made without preservatives and come in a handy, resealable bag."

By focusing your message on benefits, you'll motivate prospects to read your brochures, convince them to spend time with your direct mail pieces, and demonstrate within the first thirty seconds of a cold call that what you have is of value. We'll explore all of this in the coming chapters.

CHECKLIST

✓ What are the features of your company, product, or service? Make a long list—there may be as many as twenty-five or thirty.

✓ Translate groups of features into benefits, until you end up with a short list of about six or less. Consider intangible as well as tangible benefits, and remember, benefits always answer the prospect's question, "What's in it for me?"

✓ String your benefits together into a single, outer-directed benefit statement that will become the crux of your communications with prospects, customers, or clients.

T W O

Position Against the Competition

**Truth: A simple competitive analysis can show you
how to succeed in your own market.**

■ ■ ■

Would you dive into the ocean without any idea how high the
waves were or the depth of the water? Probably not. Suppose
you were an Internet marketing consultant and you decided to
start a home business. Could you open your practice without
knowing what to charge, the scope of the services you planned
to offer, how to position your practice, or what the expectations
of your future clients might be? Oddly enough, many home
business owners start out by making assumptions based on few
facts and figure they'll get the answers to all their questions as
they "go along." Even if you've been in your home business for
years and are continuing down a path you set long ago, you may
be making today's decisions based on outdated assumptions
about your marketing and competition.

Effective competitive intelligence can mean the difference between success and failure in your home business. It doesn't require any sophisticated tools, a research budget, or outside

vendors. All it takes is a little homework and you'll gain insight into the best way to price your products or services, available and unplumbed market niches, customer hot buttons, overserved market segments, the promises made by your competitors, and the expectations they raise for your types of products or services. These and numerous other important elements can be discovered in a competitive analysis that will help determine your ability to successfully launch and sustain your company over time.

IDENTIFY YOUR COMPETITION

The first step in a competitive analysis is to figure out who your competitors really are. The field may be wider than you think because, while you know specifically what separates your company from the scores of other businesses that offer similar services, your prospects probably don't. They may view all companies that offer similar services to yours as potential suppliers. So it's important to consider "perceived" as well as real competition and make your analysis as broad as possible.

Consider the example of one business owner, whom I'll call Sandy. Sandy does PC repair and hardware and software troubleshooting. He goes directly to his customers' homes and businesses offering affordable, on-site help as well as off-site repair with pickup and delivery. With so little competition in his immediate market area from other businesses who provided this same on-site service, Sandy thought he'd have this niche all to himself. But after six months of extensive marketing, he found his business just wasn't taking off the way he thought it would. At that point, he began to understand the effect perceived competition was having on his business.

You see, the computer superstore chain in his area also offered PC repair, though customers had to disconnect their computers and take them to the store, drop them off, and wait for days or sometimes weeks to get them back. This superstore chain was perceived competition because, even though the service itself differed in the way it was delivered, Sandy's potential customers saw the chain as a well-known name they could trust. In addition, the special offers in the chain store's ads were drawing customers in on a continuing basis. Once Sandy began to carefully follow the store's offers and use testimonials to position against their PC repair service in his own brochures and ads and on his Web site, he was able to effectively compete, particularly since his service provided a higher level of convenience and a faster turnaround time for the customer.

Here's another example. Suppose you were a home business owner who specialized in wholesale-priced team uniforms for soccer clubs. You'd have to do a competitive analysis of all companies like yours that sell custom uniforms directly to clubs, team coaches, and school athletic departments. In addition, you'd include in your competitive analysis other types of businesses, including retail stores, that customize uniforms for teams. While the pricing and delivery methods of your home business and the retail store operators would be completely different, your customers might perceive anyone who sold soccer uniforms as potential suppliers, no matter how the uniforms were sold.

▪ Gather Intelligence

Start your own competitive analysis by reviewing the Yellow Pages and other directories, making note of all competitors. Look for listings as well as ads. Go through the newspapers and magazines your target audience reads and clip all competitive ads. What are the principal benefits promised and the key selling points communicated? How often and where do your competitors advertise? What type of "call to action" is used? In other words, do they offer toll-free telephone numbers prospects may call for further information, or do the advertisers hope to make prospects take action by offering free services or special deals?

Check Their Web Sites. Contact each of your direct and perceived competitors to get copies of their brochures and other sales and marketing materials. Also examine their Web sites. These can be even more informative than brochures and ads, so you should be able to gain a wealth of information. Note how each company presents itself, and how deep (how many pages) their Web sites are. What links have they set up? Do they accept banner ads? If they're using e-commerce, which products or services are for sale and at what prices? And finally, what types of free information or help are offered? If many of your competitors have Web sites, it's a clear indication you should establish a Web presence quickly to get in the game.

Search the Internet. The Internet is a treasure trove of competitive information that makes intelligence gathering much easier than in the past. Perform searches on the major engines, such as Yahoo!, Lycos, and HotBot, for information in general product or service categories. This will turn up a host of competitive Web sites for you to explore.

If your competitors are large enough to make news or to publish new product releases or other information, you can search online news sources such as the Business Wire (www.businesswire.com), Excite (www.excite.com), and major metropolitan dailies like the *Washington Post* (www.washingtonpost.com). Best of all, you can set up your own personal news pages, which will automatically retrieve published information about specific companies, by using www.individual.com and other sites on the Web. These are excellent resources for gathering ongoing competitve information, so you'll want to check them periodically to stay current. Sandy, who specializes in PC repair and troubleshooting, might include CompUSA on his personal news page so he could stay abreast of any special offers that company made that would directly impact his own small market niche.

Mystery Shop. Once you've gathered ads, brochures, and other marketing materials, and you've reviewed articles on and off the Web and examined competitve Web sites, your next step is to contact the competitors and do a little "mystery shopping." Put yourself in the role of customer or client and go through the sales process with their personnel and, if appropriate, buy their products or use their services. This step should tell you a lot about your competitors' rates, how they charge, the range of products and services offered, and even a little bit of what it would be like to be their customer. You'll be able to judge the latter by how quickly they get information to you and whether or not someone from the company follows up by telephone.

Gathering basic competitive intelligence is an accepted business practice. But it is unethical to lead a salesperson on with promises of a big deal when you are only mystery shopping. Stay within the bounds of what you feel is honest and appropriate while gathering as much background and marketing data as possible.

▪ Analyze the Information

When reading competitors' marketing materials, try to answer the following questions:

- What are the common benefits and key selling points communicated?

- What are the types of services offered?

- Are a range of marketing niches being served, or are your competitors primarily going after one distinct type of prospect?

- What are your competitors' fees and special offers?

- What format does most of the literature take? For example, have you received mostly #10-size brochures, which fit in standard business envelopes, or are there folders with inserts?

Make Your Message Unique. All this competitive intelligence gathering will provide you with clear insight into how other businesses offer similar products or services. Here's what *not* to do with this information. Never copy a competitor's marketing materials or attempt to clone another company's business or concept. These will only result in disappointment, as every business has its own culture and unique characteristics, which, to some extent, relate to its founder. Your company, your business, and your vision will be uniquely yours. Cloning or copying another's marketing concept, even if that company is very similar to your own, will create inaccurate perceptions for your prospects and may even have legal ramifications.

The competitive information and materials will give you insight to the accepted vehicles and methods for communicating with your target audience. And they will provide vital insight into ways you can effectively mold your own product or service offering to position against the competition.

In the early nineties, my consulting firm did a competitive analysis for Marada Industries, a $60 million auto parts manufacturer and wholly owned subsidiary of an international conglomerate, to determine how best to position it against its field of competitors. After examining at least fifty information packages and brochures from the vast field of metal stamping and roll forming competitors, I was beginning to see endless images of machinery, plant equipment, and cold steel in my dreams. At first, it seemed as if it would be impossible to differentiate from the competition. But soon it became clear that what set my client apart from its field of competition was its people, and that to create marketing materials and brochures with yet more pictures of machinery and steel alone would be a mistake.

The company had grown quickly and successfully due to its emphasis on total quality management, just-in-time delivery, true empowerment, and continuous training of its workforce. These had earned Marada its customers' highest regard, and I knew these qualities would appeal to future customers as well. So the materials we created focused on the human element instead of steel and machinery, showing real people and the benefits they would bring, in order to position Marada against a sea of marketing campaigns featuring cold, lifeless materials and redundant claims.

POSITION FOR SUCCESS

In this case, a thorough competitive analysis revealed as much about what *not* to do, as what *to* do. After your competitive audit, if you see no significant difference in your product or service offering from that of the field of competitors, then you'll have to fine-tune it in order to position for success. Why launch just another "me too" kind of company? Instead, reexamine your pricing structure, delivery methods, customer service practices, even the way your day-to-day services are performed, looking for ways to provide unique client benefits. For example, one owner of a gift basket business didn't have any unique benefits to offer compared with her competitors until she decided to set up a database of all her customers' important dates and occasions. Then she could offer long-term gift programs to businesses that wished to remember their various clients on special occasions throughout the year.

▪ Niche Markets
Your competitive analysis may point to an unplumbed niche market. Before jumping in to pursue what looks like an arena free of competition, there are several things to think about. Finding a niche that is not currently being pursued can be good or bad news. First the bad news. In the past, competitors may

have gone after this niche but found it unprofitable, or the target audience may be resistant to your type of product or service offering.

Now here's the good news. If, in the past, your competitors were larger, non-home-based behemoths, they may have found this niche too small to warrant their attention. The market may have just recently emerged, or your own unique product or service offering may be the first to suit the specific needs of this unserved niche. To find out the truth, you'll have to proceed carefully. Only mindful testing will tell you whether this newly discovered field will produce a dry well or a lucrative gusher.

Sometimes the availability of a niche market can cause a home business owner to change his entire business to focus on filling a particular need. That was the case with Ed Bishop, president of Advanced Heating Concepts of Troy, New York. Bishop and his partner, Frank Lessard, saw that homeowners were embracing new radiant flooring technology that, though a bit higher in cost than other heating methods, provided a comfortable and uniformly warm environment in colder climates. By switching their company's specialty to radiant floors, Advanced Heating began selling to and servicing higher-end consumers, who were interested in the benefits of the product and were not as price sensitive as their previous clients. Bishop and Lessard could concentrate on providing a high-quality product and construction and get away from the continual competitive bidding in which jobs were awarded based on price and usually went to the lowest bidder. By shifting their specialty to radiant floors, Bishop changed the focus of the business and vastly improved his company's sales.

Your own competitive analysis may have a profound effect on the way you market your business, and it can even help you find ways to alter your product or service itself. Combine your competitive analysis with creative thinking and you'll come up with the best way to position successfully in your key market.

CHECKLIST

✓ Begin a simple competitive analysis by gathering competitive ads and literature. Look at the format of the materials, the production quality, the benefits they promise, key selling points, and special offers and promotions.

✓ Where appropriate, "mystery shop" the competition to get a real feel for the benefits a customer might enjoy.

✓ Use the information you gain to fine-tune your own product or service, or the way it's offered or delivered, in order to position against the competition and build sales.

THREE

Target Your Market

Truth: No matter how great your idea, product, or service, nobody can market to everybody. There are simply too many "everybodies" out there.

■ ■ ■

Whenever I appear on radio call-in shows across the country, I'll invariably get a call from someone, let's call him Chuck, who'll say, "Kim, I've got the greatest product on earth. Anybody can use it. Businesses can use this product, families, parents, kids. I can sell it to everybody." And I say, "Congratulations, Chuck. Do you have five or ten million dollars just to begin the launch of this product? Do you have a financial angel behind you?"—because the cost to reach "everybody" would be astronomical, particularly for a new home-based business owner.

Nobody can market to everyone. Target marketing is a way of life for companies both large and small. Even companies the size of IBM and Microsoft, with all of their marketing millions, must focus the efforts of each company division or group on a narrow audience, such as home business owners or small business owners, to minimize their waste in marketing dollars. So you can imagine how important target marketing must be to an individual home-based business owner.

Target marketing simply means to identify the narrowest possible target audience, which should consist of your best prospects, and make them the focus of all your sales and marketing efforts. Target marketing will save you time and money. According to *Sales and Marketing Management* magazine, it costs you an average of $113 every time you leave your office to call on a prospect. And that doesn't include the cost of buying the prospect lunch or traveling outside your market area for a meeting with a prospect in another city. Every time unfocused marketing efforts yield less than your best, most potentially profitable prospects, you run the risk of scheduling unproductive meetings that cost you dearly in time and money. And as a home-based business owner, the time you spend visiting unqualified prospects could be better spent doing billable work.

By narrowly targeting your market, you'll also be better able to buy affordable advertising in media that target your market niche. Direct mail is often the most frequently utilized marketing tool for home-based business owners. But it's only productive when mailed to highly qualified lists that you rent or create in-house based on a sharply defined target audience profile. The bottom line is, by using target marketing you won't waste advertising dollars to reach less-qualified prospects.

FIND YOUR TARGET MARKET

For a good example of this, let's look at the home office market itself. Just open any publication that reaches this market, such as *Entrepreneur*, *Home Office Computing*, or *Inc.* magazine, and you'll see the advertising from major manufacturers targeting this surging market.

According to the *1999 Home Office Overview*, published by leading research firm IDC of Framingham, Massachusetts, there are 4O million Americans who have some form of home office. These include people who are employed elsewhere and perform work in their home offices after hours. This work-at-home market also breaks down into several key subgroups, including:

• The 24 million people who own their own home-based businesses and operate them full- or part-time.

• Telecommuters who work for an employer and perform their work either full- or part-time out of a home office.

• The virtual office workers who, whether they work for an employer or are self-employed, must perform their jobs anywhere—hotel rooms, the front seat of a car, or a home office.

The major office product manufacturers, including Microsoft, Hewlett Packard, Canon, IBM, and Panasonic just to name a few, create products and market them to one or more of these niches. And their entire marketing approach is tailored to target a specific audience, or market segment. When marketing a product or service to other businesses, it is always important to identify your prospects by category in this way. (You'll see step-by-step guidelines in chapter 7.)

Consider the manufacturer marketing fax machines, for example. Product portability is most important to someone who must send a fax from the front seat of a car, whereas affordability may be a much more compelling feature to the full-time home-based business owner who works from the same office each day. So the same manufacturer will market a higher-priced *portable* fax machine in magazines that best target individuals who work in the virtual office environment and advertise an *affordable* fax product in magazines that most narrowly target full-time home-based business owners. The product, its marketing, and the media selected by the advertiser all change depending on which market or niche is targeted. And often, separate corporate divisions, each with its own marketing budget, are responsible for sales to these different market segments or niches.

Narrow Your Focus. If you're marketing a consumer product or service, the sheer numbers of prospects may at first seem overwhelming or too costly to tackle within the confines of the typical home business marketing budget. But once you narrow your focus through target marketing and address a specific consumer market niche or niches (more about this in chapter 8), you can undertake an affordable marketing program to penetrate that market and achieve your sales goals.

Suppose you recently purchased a household cleaning franchise. By focusing on a narrow audience, such as "women aged 35–64 with household incomes of $35,000 plus, who work outside the home and reside in [specific zip codes]," you'd reduce your advertising and other marketing costs and improve the percentage of sales you close by meeting only with qualified prospects.

Let's look at three hypothetical cases—a professional practice, a company that offers a consumer and business service, and the maker of a consumer product—to illustrate how focusing on a narrow target market can contribute to the successful launch and growth of a home-based business.

▪ Case 1: A Professional Practice

Sandra was an architect with six years' experience at a small architectural firm in Seattle where she designed residential remodels and some new home construction. Her goal was to design mixed-use residential and commercial projects for major developers in order to participate in urban renewal and preservation of community spirit in her city and others. When Sandra decided to go into her own private practice, she based her business in her loft-style living space in an old part of downtown. Her neighborhood was being reclaimed by those who, like Sandra, wanted to move back into parts of the city that had formerly been dedicated to industrial manufacturing and warehouse space.

Sandra had a strong referral base and a reputation among her circle of friends for doing good work in remodeling and renewing this type of urban residential space. So for her first year in business, she decided to make residential redesign work the focus of her new practice. To support this marketing direction, she engaged in networking activities on a social level that brought her into contact with local gallery owners, restaurateurs, and other business owners who were influencing the move back into neighborhoods like hers. She created a brochure and four-color sell sheets showing photographs of her successful redesigns for use with referral sources, including Realtors and interior designers.

Next, Sandra developed small-space ads for placement in local media, and she engaged in a well-rounded publicity program that included garnering media attention for a newly completed remodel of a former gas station into a multifunctional home and office space. She worked with a newspaper reporter as the project went through "before," "during," and "after" phases. At the end of the project, she and the new homeowners cohosted a housewarming party and invited influential community leaders and the press to show it off. To obtain national publicity, Sandra also contacted the producer of a television show that airs on the Home & Garden Television network to encourage them to cover the results of this urban renewal project in an upcoming episode.

By carefully focusing on this particular type of residential redesign, Sandra was able to position herself as an expert with highly creative ideas and gain attention on a local and national level. As a result, within one to two years, she was in a position to win the larger, multiuse projects she ideally wished to design. And over time may have the opportunity to affect urban renewal on a level that satisfies her need for participation in the community and contributes significantly to the long-term success of her practice.

■ Case 2: A Consumer and Business Service

Rhonda was a stay-at-home mom who, after the birth of her two children, was looking for a way to reenter the workforce on her own terms. She had a friend who happened to be a professional organizer, which piqued her interest, so she attended seminars, read books, and began developing a business plan for her own home-based business. Following a competitive analysis, Rhonda determined that she would leave the large corporate jobs that focused on realigning systems and communications, as well as data and files, to those with advanced degrees and expertise in that arena. She decided her primary target audience would be individuals, and that, as her business grew, she would adopt small offices as a secondary target group.

Rhonda's research showed her that individuals tend to spend much of their budget and energies on their new homes within six months following a move. So she decided to specialize in kitchen, bath, and closet organization for new homeowners. She would also assist in a move from start to finish by helping homeowners organize their belongings for the move, and creating systems for storage and organization in the new home after the move took place. With this niche and clearly defined target audience in mind, Rhonda developed programs to reach new homeowners. Instead of creating marketing materials to penetrate three target audiences—large businesses, small companies, and consumers—she developed a cost-effective program that pinpointed those prospects she believed would constitute her most profitable client base.

To reach new homeowners, Rhonda relied most heavily on direct mail to lists of new homebuyers, a referral program that offered current clients an incentive to recommend her to their friends, and participation in home shows in the local Dallas/Fort Worth area. She also polished up her speaking skills and volunteered to present a talk for local women's groups, "Ten Ways to Organize Your New Home." With this highly focused approach, Rhonda won clients in her primary target group and began to gain business from her secondary target audience—small offices—as homeowners who were happy with her work asked Rhonda to help them organize their businesses. Consequently, as her work with small businesses started to expand, she created a brochure and marketing program to reach small businesses as well as new homeowners. By partnering with subcontractors to do the installation and heavy labor, Rhonda was able to successfully expand her company and add one full-time employee to support her growing business.

▪ Case 3: A Consumer Product by an Artisan

Daniel was a dental assistant whose work making crowns led him to experiment with molding gold and silver into intricate shapes for one-of-a-kind pieces of art jewelry. What began as a hobby grew into his major interest as he sold more and more of his creations to family, friends, and neighbors. Rather than leave his job, Daniel decided to start his home-based business part-time by selling his work at neighborhood craft shows. When his silver rings, necklaces, and bracelets sold briskly at these shows, he knew he was ready to begin his business in earnest full-time.

Daniel's research showed him that most of the best craft shows required all artisans' work to be evaluated by a "jury" that selected the exhibitors. At these shows he could be assured of reaching a more affluent market, where customers would be predominantly interested in gold and semiprecious gemstones. The problem was, to appear at enough of the top shows, he would have to travel extensively. And with a new wife and a family on the way, he wanted a better strategy to reach the higher-end customer. So he created a marketing plan that included two ways to reach his target audience: through select juried craft shows and through sales to retail stores. Since both would allow him to sell the same style pieces to high-end consumers, his product line could be relatively uniform—as opposed to creating lower-cost silver rings for small craft shows and gold and gemstone pieces for retailers.

From Daniel's home office in New Jersey, he could easily participate in two juried craft shows in the region per month during warmer weather, when most of the shows took place, and focus on creating stock for retail sales and shows during the other months of the year. Sales to the wholesale market would also help offset travel expenses for shows where he sold directly to consumers. During his first year in business, Daniel met several challenges when applying to some of the better juried shows. But by year two, a higher percentage of his applications met with success.

Daniel took a two-pronged approach to targeting retail jewelry stores. He participated in to-the-trade shows where he could showcase his product directly to retailers, and he developed a prospect list with names of key stores in his geographic area. He knew he would have to modify his marketing approach for his two target audiences. Even though his ultimate buyer was the same high-end consumer, he had to develop a second, benefit-oriented approach that would appeal to the store buyers. The two principal features of his products were their uniqueness and the availability of coordinated groupings—matching bracelets, rings, necklaces, and earrings that could be sold separately or as a set, for example. This would benefit the retailers carrying his products in two ways: By carrying his beautiful and unique line, the retailer would offer customers something they couldn't find everywhere else and, because the pieces could be sold in sets, a customer would want to purchase multiple items at once or return time and again to complete a look. This would result in increased sales for the retailer.

Starting with high-quality, independently owned stores, Daniel contacted each by telephone, set appointments, and called on them one-by-one. His complete presentations were as impressive as his product and he further inspired confidence with professional-looking forms and printed support materials. By focusing on a specific consumer audience and designing a product with a unique appeal, Daniel ensured that his jewelry would sell at shows with attendees who matched his profile of a preferred customer. And because he understood the buying preferences of his consumers, Daniel was able to effectively communicate the benefits retailers would derive by carrying his product.

As these examples illustrate, no one can market to everyone. As a home-based business owner with precious time and funds, it's essential to make the most of both. Whether you're marketing to consumers or other businesses, you'll maximize your time and marketing dollars by narrowly focusing your marketing approach to reach only your best-qualified prospects.

CHECKLIST

✓ Are you trying to be all things to all people? If so, you may be hurting your chances for success. Look objectively at the products or services your company offers. How can they be tailored to appeal to your best, most profitable customers or clients?

✓ How is your focus affecting the cost of your advertising, direct mail and other marketing efforts? Are you meeting with less-than-qualified prospects? To save money and time, narrowly focus on just one or a limited number of target markets.

✓ If you're marketing to businesses, consider carefully which categories or types of businesses you will target. (There's more about this in chapter 7.) To maximize sales to consumer targets, have a clear picture of who they are and why they'll want to buy from you. You'll find a helpful method of establishing a "target audience profile" in chapter 8.

FOUR

Budget for Success

Truth: Most home-based business owners use their own money to get started, and they often undercapitalize critical areas like marketing.

■ ■ ■

Many of us have fixed assumptions about working from home that we just take for granted. Try this on for size. Imagine your same business, but in a different location. Picture yourself in a leased office space. What would your rent be? What would you do to win business? Anything you're not doing now? The only real difference between your home-based business and any other small business is location. But because many people consider home a "safe" haven, it's easy to become comfortable and complacent. You forget to run your home-based business like any other, with established budgets for key programs, including marketing.

The Small Business Administration tells us that two of the principal reasons for small business failure are undercapitalization and lack of effective marketing programs. That's not surprising, since the two go hand-in-hand. You should expect to spend at least $5,500 to set up a bare bones home office. That includes a computer and software with modem and backup zip drive, a monitor, a printer, fax machine, and telephone, plus basic furnishings. You'll need a desk and filing cabinet, plus a comfortable, ergonomic chair, and a lamp or two. Any additional software and equipment will add to this basic cost. (See chapter 5 for more ideas on technology.)

DEVELOP A MARKETING BUDGET

You should also expect to spend $5,500—or more—on marketing programs in your first year. Some home business owners undercapitalize marketing because they don't see themselves as "running a business." Do you fit this description? If so, you've adopted a dangerous mindset. Without some form of marketing, sooner or later you'll find yourself out of a "job." You see, nothing in the business world remains static for long. You may have a contract from a major company today, but your contract can dry up, that business may be acquired by an even larger one, or your contact there may change, leaving you, an independent contractor, scrambling for more work.

Your actual budget will depend on several factors:

The Size and Location of Your Market. If you plan to sell a consumer product nationwide, for example, your marketing costs will be dramatically higher than if you market a business service in your hometown.

How Difficult Your Prospects Are to Reach. Some target audiences will require greater resources and efforts to penetrate. For example, you can expect to pay more for a direct mail list of information services managers at technology companies, which is more difficult to create and update, than for a list of all residents in a particular zip code.

The Type of Marketing Tactics Required. Some marketing tactics require a larger budget than others. For instance, it will cost more to mount a television campaign to market a consumer product than it will to send four-color sell sheets to business-to-business prospects.

The Sales Tools You'll Need to Compete. No matter what kind of business you're in, your tools must be of the highest quality. But the types of tools your business requires will dictate the budget that must be allocated. For instance, a contractor meeting with homeowners might require a four-panel color brochure, pre-printed estimate sheets, and an attractive photo album with examples of completed jobs, while a high-technology marketer will need expensive equipment to make the sale, including a laptop computer, LCD projector with screen, and presentation software.

The Level of Competition in Your Market Niche. It costs more to mount a campaign to effectively break through competitive clutter than it does to communicate with your target audience in an environment relatively free of competing messages. If your market niche is filled with well-established and entrenched competitors, you'll have to employ a wider range of marketing tactics and fight hard for positioning and top-of-mind awareness.

FUNDING OPTIONS

Did you fund your start-up with a traditional business loan? Probably not. Typically, home businesses seek smaller start-up loans than are profitable for financial institutions. Simply put, lenders can't make enough money from a five- or ten-thousand-dollar loan to make the risk worth their while. Home business start-ups also have difficulty securing traditional small business loans due to their lack of significant tangible assets, such as equipment, real estate, or receivables to use as collateral. The SBA offers a MicroLoan Program, but it's primarily for start-ups owned by women and minorities in inner cities and rural areas; they're not available to everyone. Consequently, most home business owners fund their own start-ups using their savings, personal loans and lines of credit, loans from family and friends, and credit cards.

If you've started your business using your own funds, you may be tempted to cover the cost of your equipment and overlook other critical components to success, including sales and marketing programs. Businesses that use bank financing to cover their start-up costs rarely make this mistake, because to obtain a bank loan you must have an effective business plan that details important information such as: who you'll market to, why they'll want to buy from you, your sales and marketing strategies, and a marketing budget.

▪ Set Financial Goals

As I mentioned in the Introduction, home business owners have higher household incomes (about $60,000 a year) than the average American worker and a large percentage earn six-figure incomes. Marketing is an investment in the future success of your home-based business, and you should consider it an operating expense to be factored into your pricing structure. Set strong financial goals, and use sales and marketing programs to generate leads and sales that will get you where you want to go.

One rule of thumb is that you'll need to earn at least one-third more as an independent home business owner than you did as an employee to realize the same salary. (And, of course, as your business grows and you hire independent contractors or employees, the amount you project in earnings must increase proportionately.) In many cases, you can expect your marketing costs to draw against a higher percentage of your gross income during the start-up phase of your home-based business.

That was clearly the case for Ken Norkin of Takoma Park,

Maryland, a successful advertising agency copywriter who decided to strike out on his own. When Norkin started his business in 1991, he wanted to position himself as a business-to-business, high-technology copywriter who could make short work of complex assignments. He targeted advertising agencies, design studios, and select local corporations and associations in the Washington, D.C., area. Norkin decided his best marketing tool would be oversized postcards. For a start-up investment of about $1,500 dollars, he created five-by-seven-inch cards that were creative, clever, and funny, with a different card for each target audience. He sent an initial mailing of several hundred cards, and then repeated the process periodically throughout the year.

Norkin's investment was amply rewarded. Two days after his very first mailing, Norkin got a response from an advertising agency that became a client—and has been ever since. Over the past eight years, that client alone has paid Norkin *hundreds of thousands of dollars.*

But what if your start up marketing program requires more than several thousand dollars? What if you need half a million or more to reach your market? That was the challenge for the founders of Atomic Web, Inc., which created a turnkey Web site development tool for businesses and individuals called website 2 Go, which includes e-mail, a complete statistical package of tracking tools and support, as well as Web site hosting. The four partners, Steve Chambers, Lynn Van der Veer, Don Dailey, and David Dear, each of whom works from his or her own home office in the Washington, D.C., area, needed half a million to a million dollars to work on their service full-time and test a major marketing program. (Learn more about strategic partnering in chapter 25.)

The team was initially turned down for loans by several banks. But they had two things going for them. Their product was unique in the market—a dry cleaning business, for example, could use their service and have a custom site up in hours without having to write its own content—and they were in a high-tech industry, which made them attractive to entrepreneurs with venture capital. They enlisted the services of an investment broker, who helped them define their goals and arranged meetings for the team with potential investors. Ultimately, the partners secured their start-up funds by signing an agreement with an investor who was starting an incubator. The investor and the broker received stock in Atomic Web in exchange for the funding, and the partners also received stock in the other companies in the incubator. This type of arrangement encourages all members of the incubator to contribute to each other's success. With their funds in hand, the Atomic Web partners are taking website 2 Go to select markets in anticipation of a successful national rollout.

- ### Find Funds for Growth and Expansion

Once your home-based business is up and running, you'll find there are more funding options available to you. Say you've been successfully marketing your company on a regional basis for two years, and you need additional funding for growth and expansion to reach national audiences. You'll find a warmer reception from traditional funding sources, provided you're prepared to look beyond your local bank. Contact the Small Business Administration (800-827-5722) or visit its Web site (www.sba.gov) for information on SBA-backed loans, which are designed to make more credit available to women, minorities, and very small businesses. You can also search the archives of *Entrepreneur* magazine (www.entrepreneurmag.com) for its annual "Best Banks for Small Business" feature, which includes information on banks that make the largest number of loans to small businesses. You'll find Wells Fargo and Company (www.wellsfargo.com), which is actively funding small business growth and expansion, at the top of the list.

No matter whether you have outside loans or are financing your business on your own, don't let limited funds stand in your way. I know one successful home business owner who had to borrow subway fare from her babysitter to visit her first prospect. There are all kinds of creative marketing strategies that will take your business to the next level. Throughout this book, you'll find ideas and stories of home business owners who followed their own paths to success.

CHECKLIST

✓ Challenge your own assumptions about working from home. Imagine your business were based elsewhere. What would you do differently to win customers or clients? Now ask yourself if you're consciously "running a business." Are you prepared to put programs in place that will ensure your company's long-term growth?

✓ Budget the same funds for marketing you'd set aside if your business were located in an expensive office suite and you had to sign a monthly rent check. You'll find out how to set up your ongoing marketing program in chapter 21, and you'll learn the best way to write a simple marketing plan for your home-based business in chapter 22.

✓ Set clear financial goals for your business. Plan to earn at least one third more than you did in your previous job if you want to stay at the same income level. But why not set your sights higher and join the many home business owners with incomes of one hundred thousand dollars or more?

FIVE

Create a Quality Image

Truth: When you're home-based, your marketing materials become your storefront, your corps of salespeople, and your blue suit.

■ ■ ■

A budget for effective sales and marketing materials is a top priority for all businesses, but it's absolutely critical when your business is home-based. Think about it: When you base your business in your home, it's virtually invisible. You have no retail storefront, little or no exterior signage, and no army of blue-suited salespeople out knocking on doors on your behalf. Your materials are your blue suit. They're the ambassadors you send out to call on prospects.

Quality materials make a vital difference in how a home-based business is perceived. They're essential to the successful launch of your business and its growth in the long run. And they'll immediately communicate a positive impression to prospects and convey that your business is stable and permanent. Like any other businesses, small or large, there will be good and bad home-based businesses. Yet prospects will base many of their initial assessments of your firm on the impressions made by your materials—brochures, letters, direct mail pieces, and presentation tools.

The total number of businesses in America is expanding at a dramatic rate. Ten years ago, when home-based businesses were considered an oddity, there were fewer business entities overall. Now, with the proliferation of millions of home-based businesses and other small firms, your actual number of competitors may have grown exponentially. This ever-increasing level of competition in every market niche makes high-quality, effective marketing materials essential.

To start your business off right and compete toe-to-toe with home-based and larger competitors, create a cohesive family of materials that work together to create a powerful company image. When developing your materials, it's not important to match your competitors dollar for dollar. What matters most is that your brochures and other materials validate the impression of your company as solid and successful, communicate a unique set of benefits, and motivate prospects to take action.

FINE-TUNE YOUR IMAGE

Image is everything. Prospects want to make good choices. And most want to make *safe* choices too.

Let's imagine, for example, you're the head of your condominium or neighborhood association and in charge of selecting a landscape contractor for your community. Two individuals come in to see you and both give you similar bids. The first contractor hands you a business card with the telephone number crossed out and a new one written in, writes his estimate on a blank sheet of paper, and hands you a photocopied 8½-by-11-inch flyer promoting his company.

The next day, you meet with the second landscape contractor, who gives you a white folder with the name of his company printed on it in green and an illustration of a plant as a part of his logo. Inside the folder, there's printed information about his company and several case histories. The estimate he hands you is written on a form preprinted with his firm's name and logo.

Which company inspires the greater amount of trust? No matter how good the presentation was from the first landscape contractor, your gut reaction will be to make a safer choice by going with the second landscape contractor, who gives the appearance of having a stable, professionally run company by virtue of his high-quality, coordinated family of marketing tools.

PRODUCE A FAMILY OF TOOLS

Make no mistake, your own prospects will make critical decisions concerning you and your firm simply based on the quality and content of your materials, long before they have an opportunity to develop a professional relationship with you and learn the benefits of utilizing your services. So you'll need a family of materials that "get along." They must work together to create an image and support all of your sales activities. To decide which tools you need, imagine a typical series of client/customer transactions, and list all the tools you might use along the way.

For example, a business consultant will need stationery, a business card, and a company brochure to mail to prospects and use in meetings. He or she may also choose to have a folder with inserts to carry case histories or proposals, and presentation tools for group meetings, such as with the board of directors of a foundation or midlevel managers of a corporate prospect.

Here's another example. A home improvement contractor will advertise, and make follow-up calls to the leads produced from the ads. The contractor will then require tools including a brochure, business card, and an estimate sheet for follow-up meetings.

Like all business owners, the business consultant and the contractor will also need tools and materials to maintain contact with their prospects and clients on a continuing basis. These may include newsletters, copies of press releases, direct marketing packages, postcards, and other materials. And finally, they'll need contracts, invoices, and stationery with matching envelopes in a variety of sizes for ongoing correspondence.

Depending on your type of business, you may find that your family of tools has as many as a dozen components. It's easy to see how, without planning and coordination from the beginning, you can end up with a hodgepodge of mismatched pieces that convey a poor impression to your prospects and customers.

■ Production Tips

When it comes to production, there's plenty of help available from a variety of resources. Often, your best option is to contract with a designer and copywriter as a team who can work with you to create the tools you need. Your design and copy team should supply your materials on disk so that you can print them out in your own office or take the disk to a printer.

Here are two ways to save money when you use these services:

1. It's always less expensive to produce your family of materials together. If you use a designer and/or copywriter to create your materials, you'll save money by having them produce the family of tools you'll need as one project. There will be fewer meetings and phone calls and, consequently, smaller bills.

2. If you're having your materials printed in the same ink colors, then you'll also save money by printing several of your pieces together, since a sizable portion of your printer's charges are for initially "inking the press" for each job.

Create Your Own Materials. You may also choose to design many of your marketing materials on your own with the help of desktop publishing software. Just be sure to resist the temptation to overdesign (see chapter 6). Whether you design your materials yourself or have them created professionally, you should keep your stationery art, including your logo, on disk. Develop templates for materials you use frequently, including press releases, flyers, newsletters, postcards, and fax bulletins, so you have them at your fingertips at a moment's notice. This will help reduce the amount of time you spend preparing individual tools as a part of your ongoing program.

Home Office Equipment. The best way to save money and create a high impact, quality image for your business is to use a combination of materials that are professionally printed and tools that you modify in-house on a regular basis or turn out for a specific purpose, such as a major presentation. For a polished look, use a color printer and high-resolution scanner in your home office. If you're just starting your business, you have the option of buying individual pieces of equipment, such as a stand-alone color printer, scanner, copier, and fax machine. Or you can affordably purchase what are called all-in-one machines, sometimes referred to as multifunction devices. Decide what you'll be using your equipment for most, and shop accordingly. Depending on the model and manufacturer you choose, for example, one might have a lower resolution scanner but a faster print time than other machines.

You can compare prices and stats at www.computershopper. com and look for reliable reviews in *PC World* magazine online at www.pcworld.com. Manufacturers, such as Hewlett Packard and Canon, regularly update models or introduce new ones approximately every six months. So you may find a lower price on an older model that meets your needs.

As anyone who's been in a home business for some time knows, every work surface is eventually filled with some piece of equipment. If the equipment is old, outdated, or just needs replacing, an all-in-one machine may help you bring order to chaos. Otherwise, upgrade to an affordable inkjet printer that does a good job on color printing, or spend a bit more for a color laser printer. Then add a high-resolution color scanner if you regularly import photos into sell sheets, presentations, or other marketing tools.

Sue Cross, president of Cross Reference, a multimedia and technical writing and documentation business in Oak Park, California, is working on a project for the U.S. Park Service on wildfire ecology. Cross uses a digital camera to take high-resolution pictures in national parks, downloads them into her solar-powered portable computer, then erases her camera's digital disk. This way, she can keep shooting on location indefinitely.

For creators of multimedia presentations like Cross, and insurance and real estate professionals among others, a digital camera is an important tool for adding photographs to flyers, sell sheets, brochures, Web sites, and reports. But if you need to import pictures into your marketing materials only occasionally, there are less costly ways to put your photos on your computer disk. With a product from Kodak and Intel called the Picture CD, you can have your 35mm photographs processed and returned with a package that includes a contact sheet, a set of paper prints, and a CD with digital renderings of your photos. It comes with easy-to-use software that allows you to crop and improve photographs, such as by removing red eye.

Even if your equipment budget doesn't cover the purchase of a color printer, you can still produce terrific color materials from your computer. Suppose you want to present a ten-page, color version of an important presentation. You can create your presentation using software such as Microsoft PowerPoint, Corel Presentations, or Lotus Freelance Graphics, copy your presentation onto a disk, and have your copies printed out at a local print and copy center. If your presentation includes complex visuals (lots of graphics and photographs) you'll need to download it onto a Zip disk. No Zip disk drive on your computer? No problem there either. Each of the programs mentioned has a service bureau contact screen embedded in it. For example, Microsoft PowerPoint has a partnership with Genigraphics, so you can order slides, color prints, or posters made of your presentation via a direct Internet connection from the program.

Broadcast Faxing. When it comes to creating ongoing marketing tools for current customers or clients, there's another low-cost, time-saving alternative. Instead of producing your newsletter or other ongoing marketing tool the old-fashioned way—spending time and money to print or copy, fold, stamp, and mail it—you might want to consider broadcast faxing instead. With a low-cost fax software program, such as HotFax by Smith Micro, you can lay out a one- or two-page fax newsletter using a desktop publishing software program, then you only need to input your fax list of prospects or customers once, and with just a few clicks you can send your newsletter out to your entire list. You can even program the software to send your faxes out at night when there's less chance of getting busy signals. This is an excellent way to maintain regular contact with your database for minimal cost and effort. There's one caveat: Only send broadcast faxes to companies that have agreed to receive your information or who are current customers to avoid running afoul of the regulations that prohibit sending unsolicited faxes.

In all, you can use your own color printer to create sales and marketing tools, copy your materials onto disk, and have them printed out at a print and copy center, or you can use a service bureau. You can even use broadcast faxes to save time and money. Thanks to affordable equipment and services, you can now produce flyers, sell sheets, presentation tools, handouts, and other materials in your own home office.

▪ Elements of Design

All of your materials should have certain elements in common. Among them are your logo, type styles, color scheme, paper stocks, a positioning statement or slogan, and a consistent use of either photography or illustration.

Paper Stocks. Two elements that really give your materials a high-quality look are the paper stocks you choose and your use of color. Paper stocks come in varying weights (expressed as lb.) and finishes. It's helpful to select a paper stock that meets your needs and use it in a variety of weights for different purposes. For example, you might use 80-lb. cover stock for your company's principal brochure and the same stock in 70-lb. text weight for a component part of a direct mail package. By going with the lighter-weight piece for direct mail, you'll save on postage.

But beware of choosing paper stocks that are too lightweight to make a positive image when used for brochures and cards. The colorful and imaginatively designed paper stock you find in the stores may be fine for special uses as part of a stationery package, but much too lightweight to make a strong impression when used on your company brochure. The truth is, the business card stocks offered in sheets in stationery stores are too lightweight to support a professional image, and you're better off with business cards that are professionally printed.

Colors. When it comes to use of color, printers also offer dynamic paper stocks, such as those with marble backgrounds and textured finishes. These slightly more expensive papers are an asset that can actually help reduce your printing costs. You can use any one of these colorful, eye-catching paper stocks to coordinate throughout your family of materials. Then print on them in just one or two colors (instead of four), and reduce your overall cost of production.

Consider two things when choosing a color family for your

tools. Ask yourself, "What will the colors I'm using say about my business?" and "How will my target audience react to these colors?" In other words, if you're selling skateboards, it's okay to go for fuchsia, screaming red, and hot yellow, but if you're a business consultant you will be limited to the colors your target audience will find acceptable.

Colors, and their varying hues, carry specific connotations. Green, for example, signifies growth and renewal, like the coming of spring. It's also the color of U.S. paper money. Traditionally, the color blue has represented loyalty and faith, and since the beginning of the twentieth century it has been the symbolic representation of the male gender. So it's not surprising that a brochure I recently received from Janus—one of the country's leading money fund companies—uses muted bars of blue and green as a design element throughout in order to convey the impression of a venerable and stable firm that manages funds that will help its investors' money grow.

For some initial clues to the color families that will have the greatest appeal to your target audience and convey an appropriate image for your firm, refer to the materials you collected during your competitive analysis. What do the colors your chief competitors use tell you about them? And, most important, consider what the color choices communicate about your target audience.

▪ Write a Positioning Statement

Ever wonder what your company's name really says about you? If it isn't clear from your company name alone what type of work you perform or the products and services your company offers, you'll need a *positioning statement*. This is a short description of what your business does, which you'll place just beneath your company name or logo on your marketing materials. With a company name like Peabody Public Relations, you probably won't need a positioning statement. But if your firm is called Peabody and Company, you may have a problem. In order for prospects who receive your business card, brochures, and other materials to know at a glance that you offer public relations services, you'll need a positioning statement to describe your area of specialization, such as "full-service public relations for technology companies."

In many cases, you'll have just a few seconds to convey your company image to prospects. In that short span of time, they will make quick decisions about whether your firm and the information you provide will be of benefit to them. When you attend to all the essential elements, from color, paper stocks, and a positioning statement to typefaces and benefit-oriented copy, you ensure your materials make a good first impression and present the right image for your home-based business.

LOWER COSTS WITH QUALITY MATERIALS

As a final note, here's another reason to invest in your image. Quality materials can actually raise the temperature of a sale while lowering the cost of selling. Remember, it costs about $113 or more every time you leave your office to call on a prospect. But let's say instead you create a terrific brochure and marketing package that costs about a dollar apiece. Then you mail that package out to fifty prospects, and it excites ten of them enough that they agree to meet with you. If you close most of them, it's easy to see that you'll have spent considerably less money to make those eight or nine sales than if you had gone out and met with fifty prospects one-by-one and then closed nine. You would also have made those sales in less time, which means you'd have more income early on to fuel further business growth.

A cohesive family of effective tools will shorten your sales cycle, create a positive image for your business, and help increase your income in a shorter period of time. So invest in your image. It's well worth it.

CHECKLIST

✓ Mentally walk through a typical sales transaction. Make a list of all the stationery and other tools you'll need. Resist the temptation to pare down your list to the bare essentials: Include all the items, though you may postpone production of a few until your business is in a strong growth mode.

✓ Make a list of the marketing tools—from postcards and press releases to newsletters—that you'll use in the course of your annual program. Can templates for these tools be designed along with the sales materials and stationery package above? Can they be printed together?

✓ Maintain templates of the tools you must regularly customize on disk ready to be printed out in-house as needed. Use quality equipment to create color materials in your own home office.

✓ Replace your old-fashioned way of creating newsletters and other ongoing tools, and adopt broadcast faxing. With a few clicks, you can send a monthly newsletter to your entire list, instead of printing, folding, stamping, and mailing.

✓ Ensure a coordinated look for your tools by selecting a family of paper stocks and a type style that will be carried through your materials. Create a positioning statement if your company name isn't descriptive of the products or services your company provides. And finally, do a quick check to determine if the quality of your materials stands up to those of your competitors.

SIX

Build a Better Brochure

Truth: A good company brochure isn't about what you offer—it's about what your customers or clients will get.

■ ■ ■

In the last chapter, we discussed developing a family of sales and marketing materials that work as a cohesive unit. Now we'll zero in on one of the most important parts of that package: the brochure. Too many home-based business owners make a fatal mistake. They think their company brochure is just a basic information piece they send out indiscriminately when they can't get to first base with a prospect. Not so. A terrific company brochure can help you:

- Position against your competition
- Motivate prospects to buy
- Communicate your key benefits
- Direct prospects toward a specific action
- Lower the real cost of selling

- Create a visual identity for your home-based business

If you think this sounds like a tall order, you're right. That's why your company brochure is your most crucial piece of literature. It doesn't have to cost a lot, but the content and layout should be right on the money. Whether you bring in experts for design and copy or you create your brochure yourself, the two critical elements that will make or break you are the content and the design/layout.

CONTENT IS KING

You will have just a few short seconds from the time someone receives your brochure to when he or she makes a decision whether or not to keep it, read it, or immediately toss it in the trash. Each day as you open your own mail, you make instant decisions about brochures you find there. By now, you've seen hundreds, or even thousands, of ineffective company brochures. You know which ones they are. They're like the one for the management consultant that addresses only features such as, "More than 20 years' experience . . . Specializing in midsize businesses . . . Personalized, one-on-one client service," and on and on. These "inner-directed" brochures contain a litany of features that fail to draw in or motivate the reader to keep the brochure and learn more.

■ The Outer-directed Brochure
The content of your company brochure must be *outer-directed*. There should never be a focus on what "we do," "we offer," or "our experience." Instead the copy should focus on what "you'll receive," that's the benefit to the customer of your product or service. Do you remember the truth we focused on in chapter 1? "To motivate prospects and customers, you must answer their

question, 'What's in it for me?' " That's the single most important element when it comes to effective brochure copy.

Writing Effective Copy. Headlines and subheads move the reader along with benefits. They're not titles, like in a textbook. We tend to read brochures in this way: Headlines first, then subheads or photos, photo captions, and then the body copy (the text) last. So everything—from headlines and subheads through copy—must be outer-directed and answer the prospects' question, "What's in it for me?"

Here's a fictitious example of a typical, features-oriented brochure headline. This is how to do it the *wrong* way. The cover headline might read:

James Doe, Certified Management Consultant
Specializing in effective systems for midsized businesses

A better headline for the cover would be one that teases the content and motivates the reader to open the brochure and read on, such as:

Name three ways to put your business on the fast track…

Subheads, which should be sprinkled throughout the copy, must also draw the reader in. To continue with the same example, three weak subheads would be:

• Personnel studies and evaluations

• Team building programs

• Management systems analysis

Terrific brochures use subheads that spark the reader's interest. Excellent subheads win the reader over and convince him or her to read on. Replace the subheads above with these more powerful, "active" ones:

- Improve productivity in every department
- Build motivated, high-performance teams
- Adopt streamlined systems that support sales growth

The copy that follows each of these subheads must be equally outer-directed and speak to benefits first, followed by features (see chapter 1). At the close of your brochure, a strong "call to action" gives your prospect a reason to respond. An appropriate and effective call to action will depend upon your type of business and the products or services you offer. A call to action that includes a "free 30-day trial" or a "10 percent discount off your first order when you call in the next thirty days," is a great way to build an immediate response for sales of a specific product, for example. Determine what types of calls to action your competitors use in their brochures and other marketing materials, then find a way to make your offer stand out. No matter whether you offer a "confidential on-site evaluation" or a subscription to a free newsletter, the offer should be of real value and unique to your firm.

▪ Toll-Free Numbers

If you're marketing regionally or nationally, include a toll-free number to increase the responses your brochure will receive. When you fail to provide a toll-free number, you create a sales barrier because potential customers think twice before assuming the responsibility for long-distance charges to investigate an unknown. Until recently, long-distance companies charged a monthly fee per toll-free number and a higher rate per minute to smaller customers for in-bound toll-free calls. But now, some major carriers have removed these charges, and every company regardless of size can afford to take advantage of toll-free numbers in their marketing materials. It's not uncommon to see home-based business owners use toll-free numbers in their company brochures, direct marketing materials, and on their Web sites. When responses come in, they're careful to ask callers where they learned about them to help gauge the effectiveness of each marketing tool.

Consider the example set by Pacific Medical, a San Diego, California, home-based business owned by Joanne and Todd Mitchell. Started in 1989 as a medical billing company, in the last five years, Joanne Mitchell has successfully added training seminars throughout the country for those who want to start their own medical billing practices. Joanne now runs the training division and her husband, Todd, has joined her to run the billing practice with an additional employee in their home office and three independent contractors to handle the work of the two busy divisions. The Mitchells use a toll-free number in their marketing and as a customer service tool. The toll-free number is displayed on the company's brochures and Web site, and it's provided to their training graduates so they feel at ease calling Pacific Medical as often as necessary.

With the new affordability of toll-free numbers, you can use different numbers to test the results of ads placed in specific media, or the effectiveness of a particular brochure or direct mail package, just as major corporations did for many years. Interestingly enough, use of a toll-free number still carries some of its old cache and can help you convey a big-company image.

DESIGN HINTS

Like many home-based business owners, you may decide to make your company brochure the centerpiece of your family of related tools. So the design elements you use, including logo, typestyles, paper stock, and use of photography or illustration, should be carried though to your other materials.

Designing It Yourself. If you decide to design your own company brochure, chances are you'll be using a fairly foolproof software program developed for those who are not professional designers. Still, one of the most obvious design mistakes home-based owners make is to use too many different typefaces. This immediately makes a brochure look amateurish. To avoid this error, pick one typeface for text and another for headlines—and don't be tempted to use every version of the face. The key is to keep it simple. Don't overdesign. Forgo exclamation points and underlining. Emphasis in design is made with type weight (boldface, for example) and type size. Effective design and layout are easy to follow and to read, without too many boxes or extraneous elements that keep the reader bouncing around on the page.

The truth is, if you're unsure of your design capabilities, this is not the time for a "handyman special." This brochure is the most important tool your company has. If you had no electrical experience would you single-handedly rewire your home this weekend? There are just some jobs that require professionals and are well worth paying for. This is generally one of them.

Paper Quality. As mentioned in the last chapter, quality paper in an appropriate weight adds considerably to the presentation of your design. Many of the preprinted paper stocks designed to work in a home office laser or inkjet printer are too lightweight to convey a top-quality image. Be sure the paper you select isn't too flimsy or so heavy that it needlessly adds to your mailing costs. If you're working with a printer and are unsure whether the paper you've chosen will be heavy enough to make a positive impression, ask your printer to show you samples in graduating weights, such as 70-, 80-, and 100-lb. text and 80-lb. cover stock, and then make your decision.

- ■ Think "Outside the Box"

I recently spoke with engineer and oilman Gerry Calhoun who, after forty years in the industry, has founded New Paradigm Exploration Services with partner James Hawkins. In a brilliant move, their company has licensed CIA-developed technology and modified it so that, according to Calhoun, it will revolutionize the way oil companies search for oil by reducing the cost and increasing the accuracy when testing potential drilling sites. When developing their company brochure, Calhoun and Hawkins went through all the steps you just read about, from creating the right kind of copy to working with professional designers to get an effective design for their new brochure. Bear in mind, their company brochure must help them overcome a number of significant challenges. This is brand-new technology that will require a (hopefully short) education curve for their prospective clients and ultimately a leap of faith. For those reasons, New Paradigm's brochure must convey a large amount of information, and at the same time it must create an image that inspires confidence and trust.

One of the best ways for their brochure to accomplish all of these goals would be to step out of the ordinary—to get away from the typical #10-size brochure and mailing envelope (standard business size) and step up to something larger and perhaps heavier as well. Six-by-nine-inch or nine-by-twelve-inch envelopes really stand out when surrounded by standard #10-size pieces. And that means they are more likely to be opened and read.

This strategy works particularly well for home-based businesses with relatively small prospect lists. When you have a small universe of prospects, each and every one becomes extremely important. In other words, if you're mailing ten thousand pieces a month, then a standard size, lighter-weight brochure is best for you. But if you mail only up to several thousand pieces per year to highly qualified prospects, then printing a larger-size brochure on a heavier stock may increase your costs only marginally, yet produce a better return on your investment.

CHECKLIST

✓ Create an outer-directed piece that speaks to the benefits your prospects will derive by selecting your firm. Resist the temptation to write words like "we offer," and instead write about what "you'll get."

✓ Use headlines and subheads that move the reader along throughout your piece. They should summarize the key benefits conveyed in your body copy (text). If the headlines or subheads you've created remind you of headings in a textbook, it's a sure sign they're off the mark.

✓ Include a strong call to action. Your brochure must inspire the reader to *do* something. It's up to you to decide what that something should be.

✓ Create a readable, clean design that makes an immediately favorable impression. Avoid the temptation to overdesign with a lot of boxes and artful effects. Keep it simple.

SEVEN

Find Business-to-Business Prospects

Truth: The best prospect lists are the ones you build yourself based on your vision of an ideal customer or client.

▪ ▪ ▪

One of the questions I'm most frequently asked is, "Where can I find prospect lists for my company?" The answer is simple. The best prospect lists aren't found—they're constructed name by name.

Prospect lists are developed differently depending on whether you're targeting other businesses or consumers. This chapter deals with building a prospect list to reach targeted businesses, and you'll find the how-to's of consumer prospecting in chapter 8. But if you're marketing to consumers, don't turn the page yet. You may have to market to both consumers and businesses. For example, mortgage brokers may consider consumers (typically future homeowners) as their primary target audience, yet they also have business-to-business prospects, including Realtors, who often recommend mortgage brokers to their clients. Remodeling contractors, architects, and designers may also target both residential and commercial markets.

For example, say you're based in a waterfront community in southern Florida and your specialty is installing custom boat docks, ramps, and seawalls. You'd have to maximize the number of qualified prospects in your immediate geographic area so you could service it without spending hours on the road. Your best strategy would be to serve small private marinas and individual homeowners—a business-to-business and consumer marketing challenge. Consequently, you would develop a business-to-business prospect list as well as a consumer marketing program.

If you're considering developing your own prospect list, you're moving in the right direction, because you've made the decision to target your best prospects and institute a systematic approach toward cultivating relationships with them. Successful home business owners don't wait for good clients or customers to find them. They make a concentrated search, carefully pin-pointing the best prospective customers, and then go after them.

Imagine you and your friend Bob get a group together to play basketball, with you and Bob as team captains. And suppose you quickly choose all the best players for your own team. As a result, you easily win almost every point. And poor Bob, well, his team never has much of a shot at success.

The same thing happens every day in business. Companies that actively identify and pursue the most desirable clients and customers often have the best chance of winning in the long run. Of course, there are some business owners who take a less direct approach. They print business cards and stationery, do some networking, and slowly spread the word about their companies without actively engaging in sales and marketing activities to woo top prospects. Sure, they win some accounts here and there, but with the hot competition for the best prospects in virtually every market niche, home-based business owners who wait for business to come to them will generally be disappointed in the quality or quantity of the work when it arrives. The principle is the same whether you're choosing teams for fun and games or the right kind of clients or customers for your home business.

DEVELOP YOUR LIST

Don't confuse a prospect list with the kind of list you use for direct mail, a marketing communications tool that typically contains thousands of names. (More about this in chapter 14.) The prospect list you're building is one you'll use day in and day out as you call on your top prospects.

The first step in developing a good list is to identify by category the types of prospects you want to target. What types of businesses are they—schools, hospitals, restaurants, shopping malls, banks? Try to keep the number of categories manageable, with no more than about six. If you're just starting your home-based business, you may want to draw on your past experience to define your categories. One PR executive who left an agency to found her own practice had experience in banking, hotels, and residential real estate. So she used these as her initial three categories and added two more that she hoped to branch into— restaurant chains and commercial developers.

Narrow Your Focus. As mentioned in chapter 3, focus is a tremendous problem for many business owners. By limiting the number of categories on your prospect list to no more than six, you'll focus on those in which you have the greatest expertise and from which you can expect to draw your best clients or customers.

As you begin to formulate your list of prospects in each category, consider other qualifying criteria that may be important to you. Instead of a broad category, such as "hotels," you might want to narrow it to all hotels with three or more stars in a specific geographic market area with full-service restaurants on-site, or all independently owned B&Bs in your market area that cater to international tourists. During your competitive analysis, you may have identified niche markets rather than a list of broad categories from which you'll draw your prospects. For example, you might have identified businesses with twenty or fewer employees in a certain geographic area, or all businesses that use networked computer systems, as your best prospects. The qualifying criteria are up to you. But adhering to them as you create your list will further focus all your marketing efforts on your ideal prospects.

■ Use Research

Your next step is to use research to identify the names of at least a dozen business prospects for each of your categories. This is a lot easier than it sounds. In this age when information is at your fingertips, you can find just about anything you need—provided you know where to look. The kinds of research you'll look for will depend entirely on the categories you've identified. When filling out your categories, you can visit a major public library to investigate business directories, such as *Ward's Business Directory of U.S. Private and Public Companies*, or industrial directories, such the *Thomas Register*. Consider contacting associations for their lists, and don't forget trade publications that cater to specific industries. If you were looking for the prominent day spas and salons in your area, for instance, you might start your research with *American Salon* magazine. Or if you wanted names of businesses in the hospitality industry, you could begin with trade publications, such as *Hotel and Motel Management*. Look for articles, lists, and ads that will provide clues.

Local organizations, such as chambers of commerce and Rotary Clubs, often publish membership lists that may be helpful. Even your local Better Business Bureau can be a source of information. Suppose you wanted to identify the top dry cleaning establishments in your city. Your Better Business Bureau might point you to dry cleaners who are outstanding members.

If you're familiar with using the Internet—and every home-based business owner ought to be—you can expedite national searches for prospect information. Many trade publications and directories are now available online with searchable archives. In addition, you can search for information on specific categories of businesses through any major search engine including Excite, HotBot, Lycos, and Yahoo!, just as you did when performing your competitive analysis. And for news items concerning specific companies, you can search on www.individual.com and www.businesswire.com, among others. If your major city newspaper is available online, like the *Los Angeles Times* or the *Washington Post*, you can also use the Web to search for information on businesses in your immediate area.

In some cases, you'll uncover significantly more than just the dozen names you want in each category. Keep the additional names on file to use as your list evolves. Over time, some prospects will become clients or be dropped from your list, and others will need to be added.

You should expect to spend a week or two pulling together this information, depending upon its complexity and the difficulty locating it. If the information you're searching for is fairly obscure—such as the companies in your market area with two hundred or fewer employees that have in-house servers—you'll probably have to use a consumer marketing strategy (more in the next chapter) and rent a direct mail list, possibly one with telephone numbers and telemarketing privileges. Then you'll add the key prospects who respond to your direct mail or telemarketing efforts to your list.

▪ Make the Right Contacts

With your list of at least a dozen companies or organizations per category in place, your next step is to call each one to get the name of the person closest to making a buying decision, and add that name to your list. It will help if you decide in advance the title this person might hold—vice president of marketing or director of purchasing, for example. Sometimes, the biggest puzzle will be deciding which department to call. A producer of corporate videos who is marketing recruitment tapes recently asked me if she should approach the personnel or marketing divisions of the prospect companies she has targeted. In her case and in many others, there's no single right answer. You may have to make a few telephone calls before you get it right, and it may vary by company.

Work from the Top Down. Here's an intriguing truth: *It's simple to start your search for the buying authority at the top of an organization and work your way down, but nearly impossible to start at the bottom and work your way up.*

Think about it and put yourself in your prospect's shoes. Imagine you are the marketing manager for a banking chain and you get a call from a public relations professional who offers to help your bank develop programs for building use of electronic banking. Based on your best assessment of the effectiveness of current programs you tell the PR person that you have no need for his services at this time. Weeks go by, and you're in a marketing meeting with your supervisor and her boss, the vice president of regional marketing programs. The VP announces he's met with a PR person and would like you to evaluate his proposal for increasing your customers' awareness of electronic banking. You're irritated and surprised to learn that this is the same PR person you spoke with a month before.

Would you be likely to give a rubber stamp of approval to the PR person's proposal, or would you find reasons not to give it your endorsement? Even if you were to go along with the group and endorse hiring the PR man, what would your working relationship be like with that individual, knowing he had gone over your head to your bosses? Get the picture? Nobody likes to be made to look bad, and everyone dislikes having someone go over their head to their boss or supervisor.

Pursuing lower-level buying authorities is a no-win situation, because even if they like what you have to say, your ability to close will be dependent on their skills at presenting your selling proposition to their senior executives and on their own clout within their organizations. That's why, though you may find it intimidating at first, it's vital to start with the most senior person in any organization you believe has the ability to make a buying decision, even if it means starting with the president of the company.

Finding the right decision maker will take time and qualifying by telephone will play a central role in list development. In business-to-business communications, the traditionally accepted contact sequence is call, mail, call. That means your first contact with the prospects on your list is by telephone. It's the best way both to establish rapport, and to further qualify them to determine if you've found the right person within the organization and whether or not the company has a need for your product or service. Today, there are fewer human call blockers (secretaries and receptionists) between you and your prospects and more electronic interference—especially voicemail.

■ Dealing with Voicemail

If it's true what they say—that only about a third of all calls are completed on the first try—then you should expect to encounter a lot of voicemail. It may help you to write down the voicemail message you intend to leave and practice it in advance. But when you make the calls, never read from a script. It can make you sound inexperienced and ingenuine.

Think of reaching voicemail or an answering machine as a fifteen- to thirty-second opportunity to leave an announcement concerning the benefits your company has to offer. Begin with an "opener" that includes an introduction of yourself and your company followed by a telephone number and your benefits as described in chapter 11. You can choose to elaborate on your benefits but don't ramble on or your message is likely to be zapped (erased without being played in its entirety). And always repeat your telephone number at the end of your message. You shouldn't necessarily expect your messages to be returned, however. Don't be discouraged. This is common and you should plan to place your calls again.

▪ Call First, Then Mail

In light of the few calls that actually get through to prospects on the first try, you may be tempted to change the contact sequence by mailing first and following up your post with a telephone call. This is almost always a bad idea. You should only mail before making a call as a last resort. When you eventually get through to prospects you've mailed to in this way, the majority won't remember having received the materials. Plus, referring to the written materials weakens your opener. Your call should always begin with a discussion of benefits, not a reference to written materials.

Faxing. If you can't get through to a key individual, instead of mailing first, why not fax? Faxing lends immediacy and tends to get through the clutter and past screeners in a more effective way than standard mail. It will alert your prospect to the purpose of your call. It will also save your company brochure and other materials for when your prospect is more likely to look at them—after you've piqued his or her interest in the benefits your company will provide.

Your prospect list is one of your most vital business-to-business marketing tools. In chapter 9, on contact management, you'll see how linking this information to a database will help you track prospects and keep your follow-ups from falling by the wayside.

CHECKLIST

✓ To create your business-to-business prospect list, identify the types of prospects you wish to target by category. Keep the number of categories you choose to no more than six. This will help focus your marketing efforts.

✓ Consider any qualifying criteria that may be important to you for each of the categories you've chosen. Is the size of a business or the number of years it has been in operation important to you? What about geographic location?

✓ Assemble a list of approximately a dozen names of businesses or organizations in each category. Make use of the vast amounts of information available to you, from major directories at the public library and lists from trade associations, clubs, and business publications to online sources.

✓ Try to decide in advance the title of the decision maker in each category who is responsible for your product or service area. Then call the companies or organizations on your list to get the name of the person who fits that title or the most senior person in a position to make a buying decision on what your company has to offer. Start as close to the top as possible and, if necessary, work your way down the ladder until you find the buying authority whose name you'll add to your prospect list.

✓ In business-to-business sales, the accepted communication sequence is call, mail, call. So you should expect to contact your prospects by telephone first, then engage in a full range of follow-up activities over time. Your call will often be intercepted by voicemail. Write down a voicemail message you'll use in a typical situation and practice it in advance. Be sure it includes an introduction of yourself and your company, followed by your telephone number and a benefit statement. Chapter 11 has examples and step-by-step instructions on how to develop a successful "opener."

EIGHT

Generate Consumer Leads

Truth: When marketing consumer products and services, public relations, advertising, and direct mail will build leads, and personal selling will close sales.

■ ■ ■

There were well over 15 million consumers (usually called residents) in Los Angeles by the end of 1996, according to the Census Bureau. During the following year, at least 68,285 of them started their own businesses!

From the moment we're born we become consumers. Whether we're purchasing diapers, Porsches, or cemetery plots, virtually every moment of every day we're using something that was at one time for sale. So it's not surprising that a large percentage of the new home businesses started each year target consumers for sales of their products and services. It doesn't matter if your home business is in Los Angeles, with its 15 million plus population, or Bismarck, North Dakota, with its nearly ninety thousand residents. By narrowly focusing your marketing efforts on a specific segment of the consumer population, you'll be able to create an affordable marketing program that motivates your best prospects.

General contracting showed up in a study published by *Inc.* magazine as the number one home-based business start-up in 1997, possibly because in most places contractors must obtain licenses, which many other types of home businesses need not do. In fact, of the more than thirty-three thousand general contracting companies launched (licensed) in 1997, 87 percent were operated from a home office. Imagine what would happen if all of these new general contractors went after the same broad consumer audiences, instead of focusing on niche markets or developing a unique set of benefits and services. A large percentage would be fighting for the same piece of the pie (sound familiar?), particularly in major metro areas, where business start-ups are the highest. The top five metro areas by gross number of small business start-ups in 1997 were Los Angeles, New York City, Houston, Dallas, and Detroit. And the metro area with the greatest number of business start-ups per hundred inhabitants in 1997 was Las Vegas, where one out of every forty-two residents started a business that year, according to *Inc.*

YOUR TARGET AUDIENCE PROFILE

With intense competition for consumer markets and the sheer number of consumers available, whether you're marketing nationally, regionally, or in your own neighborhood, it's essential to create a narrow profile of your ideal customers.

In chapter 3, we discussed the importance of target marketing. Unlike business-to-business marketers, who follow the sequence call, mail, call, consumer marketers generally rely on targeted marketing communications—using newspapers, magazines, radio, television, or direct mail—and special events to produce their leads. Personally, I don't recommend telemarketing (or cold calling) to mass lists of consumers in their homes as a prospecting tactic, because many people find it offensive and it is often so poorly executed that I believe there are other, more effective means of marketing the same products and services. If you do choose to use consumer telemarketing, however, hire a professional telemarketing firm with outbound calling centers and experience in scripting and executing your type of calls.

To pinpoint your best consumer prospects, start by writing a target audience profile. This is a one- or two-sentence description of your prospects based on demographics such as age, gender, household income, and any other criteria that will help identify specific consumers as good potential buyers. This profile is an important tool that will help you save time and money— a home business owner's most precious commodities—when buying advertising space or direct mail lists and when focusing your public relations efforts.

Suppose you're one of the general contractors who opened for business in Las Vegas. You know you need a niche or specialty, so you choose kitchen and bath remodeling based on your past experience and the competitive information you've gathered, which indicates a market for an upscale kitchen remodeler. You plan to cater to the needs of the most affluent segments of the Las Vegas population who want to upgrade their well-located homes rather than move. Since new buyers of older homes often remodel within six months of purchasing their houses, you decide to target them as well as homeowners who've been in residence many years.

Your target audience profile might read: "New homebuyers and male and female homeowners, aged 35 to 54, with annual household incomes of $100,000 plus, in [specific zip codes]."

Following the example above, write down your own target audience profile to use when evaluating individual media purchases. It will help you reduce your media costs and make the most efficient use of your marketing budget.

The principal sales tool of newspapers, magazines, and broadcast media is a "media kit." Media reps use these to sell space and time to advertisers in the same way you might use your company brochure and other literature. Since media rates are generally based on the number of people who read a publication, listen to a radio station during a certain "daypart," or watch a particular television program, the most important part of the kit for your purposes will be the circulation information for print, and viewer demographics and numbers in the broadcast kits and proposals. Your job is to compare your target audience profile with the reader-, viewer-, or listenership of the media under consideration, and to look for the best match. Chapter 15 tells you step-by-step how to evaluate individual media buys, including the three rules to help you avoid costly media buying mistakes.

LEAD GENERATION

With your target audience profile in hand, you'll be able to plan your ongoing marketing program to generate qualified leads year-round. Except for home business owners who rely on catalogues or other direct response vehicles, most who market to consumers rely on personal selling to add the "heat" to close sales. Remember Ed Bishop and Frank Lessard of Advanced Heating Concepts of Troy, New York, from chapter 2? They're the contractors who specialize in selling radiant flooring to high-end customers. It was their company's switch to this unique niche that really put their business on a strong growth curve.

Bishop and Lessard use direct mail, including a monthly newsletter, and newspaper advertising to produce leads. Along with their new focus on an upscale product like radiant heating, interpersonal selling became more important. In the past, when Bishop was doing general building and remodeling, low pricing was always a principal deciding factor as to whether he won a job or it went to one of his competitors. Now, Advanced Heating's advertising yields qualified responses from more affluent customers who are primarily interested in the benefits that are unique to the company's product. Their prospect meetings are more successful, and their business, which Bishop says was started "on a shoestring," now has two to three jobs going at any one time.

Well-targeted public relations efforts can also effectively produce leads, particularly for professionals who use meetings and personal selling to close. (More on consultative selling in chapter 10.) Barbara Schlattman, ASID, of Houston-based Barbara Schlattman Interiors, Inc., is a highly successful and well-recognized designer who has had a full-time home business since 1975. (Her own glass-walled office overlooks a golf course.) Schlattman's clients include the owner of the Houston Aeros hockey team, whose home now features extensive sports murals. For another client, her designs included a waterfall and a bathroom complete with a fireplace among its elegant furnishings. In addition to her Web page, Schlattman relies heavily on public relations, including participation in ASID showhouses, which enable her to showcase her work and generate leads that produce meetings with major prospective clients.

Mark McInturff, AIA, president of McInturff Architects in Bethesda, Maryland, also relies on public relations to build leads for his ten-year-old practice. Winner of more than one hundred design awards, McInturff has appeared on *Good Morning America* and *Fox Morning News*. He and his four employees work in a beautiful setting—a compound that includes his home and a detached office overlooking woodland and garden views. Once public relations from featured magazine articles and ensuing referrals lead prospective clients to McInturff Architects, this attractive design and a portfolio of award-winning work help to cement a client relationship. (More about McInturff and how he has used public relations to his firm's advantage in chapter 17.)

Even if your home isn't a showplace, you can put a showroom in your home. Just ask Paul Ross of Northhampton, Massachusetts. His manufacturer's rep firm, Paul Ross Associates, has sales of over $2 million a year in hydronics products, including energy-conserving products, designer radiators, and radiant heating. Ross targets consumers and business-to-business markets. For consumers, he relies primarily on special events to generate leads, including participation in five home shows a year. When it's time to close, prospective customers can visit his in-home showroom (though Ross keeps his inventory at a leased location), where he can show off hard-to-find products and meet one-on-one.

Like these home business owners, your key to success when marketing to consumers is to use marketing communications to build leads, and personal selling to add the heat to close sales. Once leads are generated, you'll add them to a database and follow the sequence business-to-business marketers use: call, mail, call. At this point, you'll be making what are known as "warm calls" because your prospects will know about your company, and its products or services, and they'll be interested in learning more. If you want to know more about how to make effective warm or cold calls, follow the guidelines in chapter 11.

CHECKLIST

✓ Make your consumer focus as narrow as possible. How would you best describe your prospects? What are their demographics? Consider age, gender, household income, where they live, and any other criteria that will impact the way you focus your media buys.

✓ Write down a simple one- or two-sentence target audience profile. Include specific demographics and other qualifying criteria.

✓ Use your profile to evaluate print and broadcast advertising opportunities. Review your target audience profile when renting direct mail lists. If you're an artisan or craftsperson who participates in craft shows, choose them carefully based on how well their projected attendees will match your target audience profile.

✓ Use personal selling to add the heat to close sales, whether it's on the telephone with prospects or face-to-face.

NINE

Manage Lists and Callbacks

Truth: You don't need a staff for contact management; you need the right system.

■ ■ ■

Suppose every morning when you sat down at your desk, an assistant rushed in and handed you a list of all the contacts you'd need to make that day, including a complete file and history record on each. Not only would you be well organized and prepared to start your day, chances are you wouldn't overlook important follow-ups and callbacks to prospects and customers. Imagine another scenario. . . . In this one, each time you communicated with a client via e-mail, you could effortlessly attach that e-mail to your client files. Or suppose whenever your business received a phone call from a current customer or active prospect, his or her number and history record appeared on your computer screen.

CONTACT MANAGEMENT SOFTWARE

This isn't science fiction; in fact, these are actual functions of inexpensive contact management software programs that can revolutionize the way you spend your time and help you increase the income from your home-based business. Contact management software is a relationship-building tool because it ensures that you have the comprehensive information you need to communicate at a moment's notice with all your customers and prospects. Part scheduler, part marketing assistant with an ironclad memory, a good contact manager will reduce the amount of time you spend administering your marketing program. It can also be helpful when producing letters, memos, and proposals, and it can take the complexity out of performing mail merges so you can quickly communicate with groups of contacts. Once you record your information in the fields supplied, you can create customized databases. For example, if your business is in Portland and you want to send a letter to all your prospects in Memphis, your contact manager can assemble that list on the spot.

What if you're a journalist who interviews hundreds, or even thousands, of people a year and you suddenly need to remember the name of someone who has key information for a story you're preparing, but all you can remember is that you met the fellow in a Chinese restaurant a year ago? That's what happened to California-based freelance sportscaster Eric Tracy, who relies heavily on his contact management program to keep track of contacts and his hectic schedule. He searched his database (where he had fortuitously noted the location of his meeting) for people he'd met at a Chinese restaurant. In seconds he had the name and telephone number of his contact.

■ Real Benefits

The ability to remember personal information your prospects share with you, such as how many children they have and what their hobbies are, is extremely helpful when building relationships. Imagine how impressed a prospect would be, six months after you'd initially spoken, if you remembered to mention something about his favorite hobby, baseball. This is the kind of information people have been recording on paper call reports, on three-by-five-inch cards, and in Rolodexes for years that can be available instantly at your fingertips.

Contact management software keeps you organized. It lets you view your calendar by day, week, or month, replacing other types of less comprehensive programs. You can log in calls, meetings, to-do lists, prospect lists, marketing responses, letters, faxes, and e-mail messages. Instead of having a full-time human assistant who rushes to your desk each morning with your tickler list of follow-ups and to-do's, your software never takes a lunch break or sick day (hard disk crashes and other tragedies excepted). Most importantly, you can use this software to schedule the steps in your marketing strategies, record prospect information, maintain databases, and evaluate the results of your marketing programs. You can also manage separate customer and prospect databases, or databases of customers for different product lines, and so on.

- Evaluating the Software

At this writing, the two most popular contact management programs are ACT! and Goldmine. The newest versions, 4.0, provide telephone integration, which gives you instant access to customer and prospect information based on caller ID. ACT!, the granddaddy of contact management programs, is a good choice if you're working solo in your home-based business, and many people find it easy to use right out of the box without additional training. Goldmine was designed to be more workgroup focused, so if you have several people working in your home-based business and you want them to share information on their PCs, Goldmine may better suit your needs. However, ACT! can also accommodate multiple users.

Regardless of the type of software you choose, there are four questions to ask when evaluating a contact management program.

- *Is it easy to use?* You should be able to start using at least the basic functions of the program right away. With your time at a premium, you want a program that makes your job simpler. If the program's not immediately comprehensible, you won't use it. And with contact managers, what you get out is in direct proportion to what you put in.

- *Will it integrate with other applications?* The best programs give you easy access to e-mail and your own word processing applications (if you don't want to use the built-in processors) from inside the programs, so you don't have to launch them separately.

- *Does the program offer security?* Look for programs with integrated zipped backup (ones that send your data to your computer's zip drive). Some have special reminders when it's time to back up your files.

- *Can the program expand as you add staff?* You don't want to have to scrap your current program to adopt one that accommodates more users. A major data headache! So buy one that's expandable to grow with your business.

A MANUAL CONTACT MANAGEMENT SYSTEM

Even if an electronic program isn't for you, it's still vital to maintain some form of contact management system. If you're well organized and diligent, a paper system can perform a few of the same chores. Here's what you'll need:

- Call report forms.

• An alphabetically tabbed binder.

• A fold-out tickler sheet with boxes for each week of the year so you can cross-reference follow-ups by date. *Or* a calendar that includes lots of space for to-do lists and call-back listings, plus appointments.

■ The Call Report Form

A call report form should be completed each time you speak with a prospect. Since no two businesses are exactly alike, call report forms differ widely depending upon the information they're designed to record. Most are a single page and organized in three sections: the basic prospect data; qualifying information; and action to be taken.

Basic data on a business prospect, for example, should include the individual's name and title, company name, telephone and fax numbers, and e-mail and mailing addresses. Then leave blocks of space to fill in any important qualifying info. Suppose you're a marketing consultant. Your call report form might include space to note qualifying information, such as a prospect's current agency, their annual marketing budget, and the type of communications they use.

The final section of your call report involves action to be taken. Make it simple by incorporating boxes you can quickly check off for the next steps you plan to take, such as for meetings and follow-up calls (leave space to note the dates and times), mailing company brochures and other literature, and so on. Print out copies of your call report form and three-hole punch them. As you complete the reports, add them alphabetically to a binder.

■ The Tickler Sheet

Now here's the important part. Either you must have a comprehensive calendar system in which to note the date on which the next scheduled action step is due, or you can create a fold-out tickler sheet to go in the back of your binder. To create your tickler sheet, use eleven-by-seventeen-inch paper, printed so it folds out horizontally. On the left side of the sheet, have ruled spaces where you'll list the name of each prospect company as you make contact. On the right two-thirds of the page, you'll set up an annual calendar with a vertical column for each week of the year.

This is how it works: When you complete a call report, you'll file it alphabetically in your binder. Let's say you've just spoken with a prospect whom you've agreed to call back during the week of March fifteenth. On the left side of your tickler sheet, you'd write the name of the prospect in the next available space, and then moving across the sheet to the right, you'd put an X in the box that corresponds to March fifteenth. This way, every Monday, when you sit down at your desk, you can refer to the tickler sheet and, by looking from top to bottom, see all the companies that are due for follow-up that week. By referring back to the call reports, you'll know exactly what type of follow-up is due.

If you don't feel comfortable creating a tickler sheet of this kind, you can maintain the same sort of cross-reference system using a calendar, but it will involve a lot more writing and take greater effort to maintain. By using a simple tickler system, you can see immediately which prospect companies require follow up and then schedule your time to take the appropriate action throughout the week.

TRACKING RESPONSES

Your ongoing marketing program will generate leads on a continuing basis, and you should have your system in place when responses come in. Then you'll be ready to analyze the results of your program and move your prospects smoothly through the selling cycle. Be prepared to track all advertising, direct mail, and public relations responses. Ask every caller where they heard about your company and include this information on a call report form or in your database. And be meticulous in recording it. For example, if a prospect says she's calling in response to your ad, find out which ad and when it ran. This is invaluable data for modifying your marketing campaign and should be evaluated at least every six months to refine your marketing plan until it includes only those media and methods that produce results.

▪ Key-coding and Other Techniques

Other means of tracking advertising responses include key-coding ads, varying your product or service offer, and even using different telephone numbers to measure responses. A key-code is a small code included in your response mechanism that tells you exactly which media generated the most responses. You can key-code direct mail response cards by including a department number in your return address, for example. Or key-code your ads with a specific operator number or other code that helps you recognize the source that generated the response.

Where appropriate, you might try varying your company's offer to measure which produces the greatest response in specific media. If your home office has several telephone lines, you can feature different toll-free phone numbers, so that the responses generated by a specific campaign will be easily recognizable by the line on which they come in. By customizing the voicemail or outgoing message on that line, you'll have a complete turnkey system in place to handle incoming calls from a particular source.

The truth is, the smaller your company, the greater the likelihood that sales contacts and marketing tactics will be overlooked or abandoned when things get hectic. Contact management systems help keep you on track, streamline processes, save you time, and give you that little edge you need to stay on top of the 1,001 things that pile up when you wear lots of hats.

CHECKLIST

✓ How are leads, responses, and marketing activities tracked in your business? Do important action steps sometimes get overlooked or postponed? Evaluate the major contact management software programs to determine how they can help you streamline your processes and increase your sales.

✓ Set up a contact management system, using software or paper, to keep you on course.

✓ Begin tracking all the marketing responses you get by their source. Try using key-codes to make it easier to determine where responses come from. Include this information in your database and use it to evaluate your ongoing program.

Master Consultative Selling

Truth: To successfully close sales, you must uncover and fill needs in a friendly, noncombative, and supportive way.

■ ■ ■

Many people who've never been responsible for making sales have a negative opinion about selling. That's because the first image that pops into their minds when they think of a salesperson is someone who calls you on the telephone at dinnertime, mispronounces your name, and without pausing for breath launches into a scripted reading about a product or service in which you have little or no interest. All the while, pots are boiling over on the stove or the pizza guy is ringing the bell, the kids are crying for dinner, and the dog is sitting there pathetically holding his empty food dish. As a reward for the caller's shoddy efforts, you'll most likely hang up in his or her ear or mumble some excuse to get off the line.

Fortunately, while this type of sales interaction may have affected our image of the selling process, it's not a true reflection of what a sales interaction between you and your prospects will look or sound like. To understand why, let's examine some of the problems with that close encounter of the telemarketing kind.

First, your dinnertime caller had no clear idea whether or not what he or she was offering would meet your needs. True, your name was on a list of people who fit some of the loose criteria for a buyer of their type of product, but the caller didn't take the time to discover what your own individual needs and preferences might be. (Heck, he didn't even bother to find out how to pronounce your name properly.) The caller's second mistake was failing to determine if he had reached you at a convenient time and whether at this particular moment you might have an opportunity to consider what he had to offer.

Another fatal mistake was reading from a script, which at best makes the caller appear inexperienced, and at worst makes you feel like an unimportant, faceless, nameless number picked out of a hat. When it comes to selling, one size definitely does not fit all. And the caller has failed to recognize that. (More about this in the next chapter.)

This is not to say that all telemarketers make these glaring errors, and there are some terrific and experienced telemarketers in the field. The problem is, with such high turnover in these jobs, most of us get calls from folks who are too new on the job and perhaps too poorly paid to get it right. Look at it this way: Instead of fostering negative stereotypes about selling, callers like the one I've described should teach us valuable lessons about what *not* to do when promoting our own businesses.

CONSULTATIVE SELLING

To achieve success as a business owner, it's vital to get past the negative stereotypes of selling and study the framework of a selling style that fits your personality and is based on sound principles that, with each interaction, moves prospects closer to a buying decision. In *consultative selling*, you uncover and fill your prospects' needs in a friendly, noncombative and, supportive way. This form of interaction comes naturally to most of us and is particularly easy to master when you're passionate about what your company has to offer. Consultative selling is what you practice when you meet a prospect at a business function or for an appointment, and every time you speak with prospects or customers on the telephone. So before you ever meet with a prospect or make a cold or warm call, you'll need to fully understand the principle.

▪ Closed- and Open-End Questions

To properly fill your prospects' needs, you must uncover what those needs are. The most effective way to do this is by asking the right questions and listening carefully to the answers. It starts to get a little complicated when you consider there are actually two types of questions—closed- and open-end. Closed-end questions are fact-finders. They may be answered with "yes" or "no" or a fact. Open-end questions reveal the emotions behind the answers. They are thinking, feeling, finding questions. All of us use closed- and open-end questions in our normal conversations without giving it much thought. Closed-end questions can draw out a reticent person. They're handy for beginning and ending conversations, while open-end questions may be used for just about everything in between.

If you were having a conversation with your neighbor's five-year-old, Amy, you'd probably begin by asking a closed-end question to draw her out, such as "How old are you, Amy?" If she were to put up five chubby fingers in response, you might be encouraged to continue, and ask another closed-end question, "Do you go to school?" Perhaps you'd follow that with, "What's your teacher's name?" Once you had the child talking, you'd naturally use an open-end question such as, "What do you like best about your teacher?" To which Amy might supply all the things she likes about her kindergarten teacher. And if you were listening carefully, you'd learn a lot about Amy in the process.

This conversational structure is repeated daily in all our interactions. In a business situation, closed-end questions are ones like these:

- How long have you been in business?

- Who is your present supplier?

- At what times of year do you buy?

- Are you the person responsible for making a final decision?

Open-end questions, which can reveal a lot more detail, are ones like the following:

- What do you like best about your present supplier?

- How has the downturn in your market area affected your purchases of my type of products?

- In what ways is your business affected by overdue deliveries?

The trouble is, if you're new to sales, you may become uncomfortable when you initiate conversations with prospects, particularly if you haven't met them before. Then you may fall into what you feel are "safe" speech patterns. What's fascinating is that, in unfamiliar situations, men may tend to rely more heavily on closed-end questions, and women will use open-end questions. Not surprisingly, a man who becomes uncomfortable in a selling situation and relies on closed-end questions will have better luck if he happens to be speaking with a male prospect. So too, a female business owner will meet with less resistance if she uses predominately open-end questions with another woman.

But here's where inexperience can get you into trouble. Let's say a male computer consultant is calling a female prospect on the telephone. They've never met before, so this is their first opportunity to build a business relationship. Consequently, there's more pressure on this fellow to achieve some success on this first cold call. He begins asking a series of closed-end questions ("Are you the decision maker? . . . How long has your company been in business? . . . How many computers do you buy each year? . . . Are your computers on a network? . . . Who do you buy from now?") And he continues on in this vein, asking one closed-ended question after another. Pretty soon, he can sense his female prospect is irritated and trying to get off the line. She feels like she's being given the third degree. To her, this isn't a conversation, it's a test! And the consultant has alienated a well-qualified prospect.

Now let's imagine a female landscape designer is meeting with a male homeowner who wants a redesign of his suburban lot. This home business owner is a creative thinker. In an effort to draw out the homeowner, she asks an initial closed-end question or two, such as, "On which side of the house would you like the driveway?" Then she launches into a series of open-end questions, which she believes will help her bond more readily with her prospect as he reveals the emotion behind his vision for the new outdoor space. She asks him to describe the feeling he wants the space to evoke and asks how he feels about the use of white in the landscape. Soon, the prospect begins to roll his eyes and back away from the designer in response to each open-end question. He's thinking, "This woman is so personal and emotional. . . . I don't even have to answer these types of questions for my wife!" He labels this designer as "too creative" and finds someone else with whom he feels more at ease. Had the landscape designer used more closed-end (fact-finding) questions, the outcome might have been quite different.

If you had been one of the home business owners in either of these examples and you didn't know about open- and closed-end questions, you'd be scratching your head wondering what in the world went wrong. Consultative selling is about uncovering and filling needs in a way that makes the prospect or customer feel supported and understood, so it's vital to practice using both open- and closed-end questions in business conversations until you can use them easily, whether you're on the telephone, in a meeting, or any other situation. Practice is particularly important if the idea of selling one-on-one makes you a bit uneasy. The goods news is, once you've mastered varying the types of questions you use, you'll relax and all prospect interactions will feel easier and more comfortable for you.

Right now, think about all of the basic information you need in order to qualify a prospect, and make a list of the closed-end questions that will elicit this information. Don't stop until you have at least ten or twelve. When you have about a dozen closed-end questions written down, your next step is to loosely translate each into an open-end question. It's only a matter of rephrasing the questions. Don't try to be too literal. For example, the closed-end question, Who is your present supplier? may be rephrased as the open-end question, What do you like best about your present supplier? Notice how the open-end questions you create seem to follow logically from the preceding closed-end questions? In a normal business transaction, if you were to ask someone, "Who is your present vendor?" and she replied, "Acme Supply Company," a logical follow-up question might be, "What do like best about Acme?" It's simple once you get the hang of it.

▪ A Ten-Minute Exercise

One way to become proficient at framing open- and closed-end questions is to practice with a partner. Try this exercise. For five minutes, ask your partner a series of closed-end questions. No need to be too fussy about the content of the questions, just have fun with it. After you state each closed-end question, your partner must rephrase it as an open-end question. This is basically an exercise to help you practice framing and asking questions, so tell your partner not to supply answers—just questions.

After five minutes, switch and have your partner ask closed-end questions and you rephrase them as open-end questions.

In a total of just ten minutes you'll begin to feel more at ease with the process, and you'll have taken a major step toward ensuring your success when working with prospects.

CHECKLIST

✓ Imagine yourself in a typical cold call or first meeting with a prospect. What information will you need in order to decide if the prospect is a good potential customer or client for your home business? Make a list of the kinds of information you'll need, such as the prospect's annual sales, the name of their present vendor, their annual budget for your type of products, and so on.

✓ Write down about a dozen closed-end questions that will help you uncover the information you need. Remember, closed-end questions can be answered with "yes" or "no" or a fact.

✓ Practice rephrasing your list of closed-end questions as open-end ones. This will give you an alternate means of gaining your qualifying information and give you a handy group of follow-up questions that will reveal deeper levels of information and provide insight to your prospects' thinking and decision-making process. This is an important step in uncovering and overcoming objections. (More in chapter 11.)

✓ Practice using open- and closed-end questions with a partner until you feel at ease using both types in potentially stressful interactions, such as cold calls and first meetings.

ELEVEN

Warm Up Cold Calls

Truth: Everyone hates cold calling—until they're good at it.

■ ■ ■

Sometimes when I'm speaking at national conferences and small business expos, I like to ask the audience, "How many of you hate cold calling?" At first, just a few hands go up. And then in front of me there's a sea of hands going up as hundreds of people admit they hate making cold calls. In fact, they hate them so much, they'd raise both hands if they weren't afraid of looking silly. That's how much cold calling scares the uninitiated.

It's true. If you think of your cold call as a pitch, you're going to dread it. But when you practice *consultative selling* (which, you'll recall from chapter 10, is uncovering and filling needs in a friendly, noncombative, and supportive way) a cold call, a follow-up warm call, or any contact with a prospect is just another opportunity to help someone achieve his or her goals by buying your product or using your services.

During the same conferences and events, I ask people why they started their own businesses. The idea of being in control of their own lives and work is always an overriding factor, but there's also the belief that *they alone can do what they do better than anyone else*. There's always some new wrinkle, no matter how subtle, that the home business owner strongly and firmly believes is an improvement over what others are doing or providing. When you're this passionate about what your company sells, it's contagious. It's only natural to want to communicate how you can help prospects or customers achieve their goals.

And that's the difference between "pitching" someone and filling his or her needs. The challenges lie in learning the best ways to communicate that what you offer is of value; in uncovering your prospect's individual needs and requirements; and in reaching agreement on how what you offer can be provided within the constraints of the buyer's time frame, budget, and all the other criteria that affect his or her decisions.

Telephone calls to prospects are a necessary part of business life, and virtually every type of home business owner must make them. You can't sit by the telephone like a shy teenager on a Friday night waiting for it to ring. Otherwise, like that teenager waiting for a potential date to call at the eleventh hour, you're liable to end up working with (though hopefully not *dating*) less than ideal clients or customers, while the most desirable accounts go to those businesses that heartily pursue them.

GETTING PREPARED

Before you pick up the telephone to contact a prospect, write down a statement of purpose. What are you trying to help your client or customer achieve? A statement of purpose begins with, "My purpose is to help my client/customer . . ." This is where you put the benefit statement you developed in chapter 1 to good use. Pick out the key benefits you feel will apply to your prospect before you ever pick up the phone, and repeat your statement of purpose. Ask yourself what this person or organization needs from you and what unique benefits you can provide. If you were a PR professional calling on an organization that raises funds for AIDS awareness and research, you might have a statement of purpose such as, "My purpose is to help my client create grass-roots awareness that will affect legislation to improve the lives of those living with AIDS, and mobilize campaigns aimed at prevention of the disease among youth."

▪ Set a Strong Goal

Set a primary goal for each prospect call based on what you would most like to see happen. Will your goal be to secure an appointment, gather information for an estimate, or close the sale for a particular product? No matter what goal you select, be certain it moves the prospect to the next level in the buying process. Avoid setting weak goals, such as simply laying the groundwork to send your company literature. This is fine as a secondary, or fallback, plan if you can't achieve your primary goal during the call, but you should strive for more significant forward motion with each prospect contact.

For example, let's say Susan is an independent mortgage broker who specializes in jumbo mortgages. She lives and works in an area where most of the homes are high-priced and a large segment of the home-buying population must rely on jumbo mortgages. She's calling the sales manager of a real estate office in her area. Susan's goal is to persuade the manager to allow her to make a presentation at an upcoming weekly sales meeting. Although ultimately homeowners decide which mortgage company to choose, often Realtors play a major role in directing their customers toward a particular loan officer or company. So it's important to Susan to present more than just information on the ins and outs of jumbo mortgages at the sales meeting. She must also establish herself as an expert in the arena who will provide reliable service with no surprises that can delay closings—every Realtor's nightmare.

Susan creates a different statement of purpose when she prepares to call the real estate manager from the one she uses when she calls on potential homebuyers. In this case, she might write, "My purpose is to help my customers [the real estate agents] with dependable assistance for every homebuyer; good rates combined with knowledge and expertise in jumbo mortgages; ongoing, up-to-date information on the progress of each transaction; speedy service; and glitch-free documentation and handling to eliminate last minute problems at closing time."

MAKING THE CALL

■ The Opener

Once fully prepared, Susan can make the call to the real estate office manager. A typical call sequence will include an opener; both open- and closed-end questions; case histories and paraphrasing; and a close.

A good opener should consist of an introduction of yourself and your company, and an opening benefit. Here's an example of what Susan's three-part opener might sound like: "Hello. This is Susan Doe, president of Doe Mortgage, which specializes in jumbo loans for more affluent homebuyers. [*Pause for acknowledgment.*] My special reason for calling today is to tell you and your sales associates about the new lower rates and guidelines on jumbo mortgages that will help you increase sales from buyers in the top price ranges."

As you can see, your most important task is to communicate benefits in the first few seconds of your call. So refer to your benefit statement when developing your opener, and adapt it based on the individual needs of the prospect you're calling.

■ Getting the Prospect's "Permission"

By its nature, a telephone call is an unscheduled interruption. It's important to demonstrate respect for your prospect's time by getting permission to continue with the call, no matter whether you're calling a consumer at home or you're a business-to-business marketer contacting a corporate buyer. One of the best ways to accomplish this is to ask the question, "Did I catch you at a good time?" (Never say a *bad* time, always a *good* time.) I've tried many variations on this phrase over the last twenty years, but for some reason, this is the one that seems to put the prospect most at ease and demonstrate respect for his or her time. I have no scientific report to prove it works; I just know that it does. Most often prospects will respond, perhaps with a chuckle, that it's never a good time but to go ahead and continue anyway—*if* you've communicated within the first few seconds of your call that what you offer is of value or special interest.

▪ Asking Questions and Listening

The body of your conversation will consist of asking questions and listening to the answers. You know from reading the last chapter that closed-end questions are conversation starters. The initial closed-end questions you use will vary depending on your type of product or service. For Susan, the mortgage broker, the initial closed-end question might be, "In this area, jumbo mortgage customers make up a large percentage of the customers for your sales associates, don't they?" (Susan knows the answer will be "yes.") If the real estate office manager is particularly reticent, she can ask another closed-end question to help get the conversation started. If not, she can move right into an open-end question that will help her understand the needs of this sales manager and her agents, such as, "What are some of the difficulties your sales associates encounter when dealing with jumbo mortgages?"

When your prospect is doing most of the talking, it's a sure sign your call is going well. You've probably guessed by now that listening is really the most important part of any cold or warm call. If Susan continues asking questions in this vein and listens carefully to the responses, she will get clear insight to the ways she can help this manager's sales associates achieve their goals. In addition to asking good questions, she must also supply helpful information to illustrate the ways she can assist the sales associates solve some of their challenges. This will put her much closer to her goal of being invited to address the entire sales force.

OVERCOMING OBJECTIONS

■ Using Case Histories

Case histories, or stories, are great tools for demonstrating your company's abilities and overcoming objections. For example, if you have a prospect who is concerned about receiving on-time deliveries, she or he will be encouraged by hearing a story of how your company's on-time guarantee has been beneficial to other customers in the past—particularly if those customers are your prospect's competitors. Using case histories won't necessarily make your prospects sign up with you on the spot, but it will certainly get them thinking, and over time they'll begin to understand that the benefits of working with you outweigh those of continuing with their present supplier or contractor.

Write down four to six single-paragraph case histories that illustrate each of the key benefits your company provides. This is easier if you've been in business for a while. But even if you're just starting your home-based business, you may have stories of the ways you've previously solved problems that you can adapt for this purpose. Memorize these stories and be prepared to discuss them whenever the situation calls for a demonstration of your firm's ability to meet a specific need.

A big mistake inexperienced business owners make is to throw in the towel the minute they learn their prospect is working with one of their competitors. As you'll see in chapter 13, finding out your prospect is working with a competitor is good news, not bad, since it means they meet the principal criteria for a good prospect. When you find that a prospect is working with a competitor, it's the perfect opportunity to use a case history to illustrate the benefits of working with your firm instead.

▪ Paraphrasing

One of the best ways to demonstrate that you understand and can relate to your prospect's desires and objections is to use paraphrasing. And if you accuse me of asking you to imitate a clichéd radio shrink, I'll remind you that one of our most important needs as humans is to feel we're being heard and understood. Use paraphrasing when overcoming objections to show empathy for your prospect. Examples of handy lead-ins to use when paraphrasing are: "It sounds as if . . ." and "What I hear you saying is . . ." Some typical endings are: ". . . isn't that right?" and ". . . wouldn't you?" For instance, if your prospect has told you that late deliveries have handicapped his company's ability to fill its own orders on time, you might paraphrase by saying, "It sounds like those late deliveries have caused real problems for you, haven't they?" In addition to helping build a bond between you and your prospect, it will prompt your prospect to respond positively, such as by saying, "Yes, late deliveries have been such a headache for us."

▪ "Just Suppose . . ."

Once your prospect's objections have been revealed and you know what his or her needs are, the ways you can fill them should be relatively clear. A great method for combining case histories with paraphrasing is to use "just suppose" questions. To continue with the same example, the prospect has told you that late deliveries have caused significant problems for his company. In response, your best option is to use a case history that demonstrates how your on-time delivery policy continues to benefit your customers. Then end with a "just suppose" question such as, "Just suppose your company could get guaranteed on-time delivery or your money back . . . you'd like that, wouldn't you?"

CLOSE FOR YOUR GOAL

Let's put it all together. By this point in your telephone call, you have communicated the initial benefits of hiring your firm in the three-part opener. You've fully qualified your prospect by asking open- and closed-end questions to uncover his or her needs, and you've listened attentively to the answers in order to paraphrase and use case histories to fill them. Now it's time to close. Studies continually point out that countless sales are lost because, at this juncture, people simply fail to ask for the business. Focus on the goal you set prior to making the call, and use (what else!) a closed-end question such as, "Other than on-time delivery, are there any other principal concerns you have regarding my company's services?" If there are indeed other objections or concerns, it's time to address them.

In the end, you'll use a closed-end question to achieve your goal. If your goal is to secure an appointment, name a date and time ("Is Tuesday at three o'clock a good time for us to get together?"). Always set at least a tentative appointment, even if the prospect asks you to call back and confirm it. If the prospect says something like, "Call me next week, and I'll check my schedule," suggest that he or she at least "pencil in" the meeting. Otherwise, the following week when you call again, you'll have to repeat this entire process, and you may not be as successful on the second try.

If you can't close for your primary goal, fall back on your secondary objective, such as to send your company literature. Since it takes approximately eight contacts with a prospect before most sales are closed, it's not unrealistic to expect that it may take weeks, months, or even years to close some of your most desirable prospects. At the end of your call, make certain it's clear what specific action you'll take and be diligent about following through. This is why it's so important to have contact management software in place to keep follow-up activities from falling through the cracks.

As you practice these techniques, cold and warm calling will become second nature to you and your anxiety will pass. In the beginning, write down a good opener and have it handy. Put your case histories right where you can see them until you have them well memorized. (Though always avoid reading from a script.) And above all, let your enthusiasm for the ways you can help your prospects shine through—because passion is contagious.

CHECKLIST

✓ Visualize a typical prospect. Then write down a statement of purpose that summarizes what you'll help this particular client or customer achieve.

✓ Decide what your primary goal will be for cold or warm calls to the prospects on your list. Be certain that once you achieve this goal you'll have made a significant step in moving your prospects closer to a buying decision. Set a fallback, or secondary, goal for when you can't achieve your primary objective. Have a tickler system in place that will remind you when follow up is due.

✓ Write down a good three-part opener that includes an introduction of yourself and your company, and an opening benefit.

✓ Think about the ways you've solved problems for customers or clients in the past and write down four to six case histories that illustrate each of the principal benefits your company provides. Practice using paraphrasing with lead-ins and endings that help you weave case histories into your conversation.

✓ Decide which closed-end questions you'll use to close for your goal. Most of all, remember to relax and let the enthusiasm for what you do shine through!

TWELVE

Write the Perfect Letter

Truth: Sales letters are simple once you learn to stop writing about "me" and start writing about "you."

■ ■ ■

Every home business owner at one time or another needs a terrific sales letter. Whether it's to accompany an important proposal, to follow up on a conversation with a top prospect, or to work as a generic cover letter for company literature, the common sales letter is the workhorse we rely on to get the job done. The problem is, many home-based business owners with little experience in sales or marketing find writing sales letters an ordeal.

SIX RULES FOR SUCCESS

You don't have to earn a degree in journalism or be a professional writer to create a sales letter that motivates prospects. Here are six handy rules that take some of the mystery out of creating letters that get results.

- ## Rule #1: Set Aside Enough Writing Time

One of the biggest reasons business owners become frustrated with sales letters is they mistakenly believe writing them should be easy and quick. Don't assume because you've worked for an hour on a letter and it isn't perfect, that you lack the ability to get the job done or there's something "wrong" with you. Professional copywriters know that sales letters require careful and deliberate crafting, and if you're new at it, you should expect to spend some time perfecting your own group of letters. After twenty-two years of practice, I know it will take me about five hours to write what I consider a solid sales letter.

That doesn't mean each time a sales letter goes out, five hours have gone into its preparation. Quite the contrary. To make the most efficient use of your time, create several letters to meet different requirements, maintain them on your computer, and customize them as necessary for each intended recipient. For example, you might have one sales letter that can be customized to send to prospects who have requested information, a second to accompany proposals, and a third for cold prospects you can't reach by telephone.

- ## Rule #2: Make Every Letter Outer-Directed

The fact is, unless you're writing a letter to your mother, no one wants to read all about you. Sales letters must focus on what your prospects "will get" not on what you offer. As a novice sales letter writer, you may be tempted to effusively detail your company's credentials and all the wonderful services you provide. But unless your language is outer-directed, your prospects' response will be, "So what?" You can detail all the aspects of your product or service and why it's superior, so long as you first address the benefits prospects will receive, then describe the features that will enable your prospects to achieve those benefits in a way that answers their question, "What's in it for me?" This was the focus of chapter 1.

- **Rule # 3: Use Benefits, Followed by Features, to Make a Strong Case**

In the first chapter, you created a benefit statement and I promised this would become the crux of everything that was read, heard, and seen about your company. Now, with your benefit statement in hand, you're halfway home. To prepare your sales letter, make a list of the principal benefits the recipient will receive, and weave them into your opening paragraph. If your letter contains a special offer, that will become part of your opening hook. In addition to your principal benefits, your special hook will draw in the reader and entice him or her to read further.

Following your opening paragraph, the body of your letter will use features to illustrate how the reader will take advantage of the special benefits your company offers. If your principal opening benefit offers to help your prospect's company increase its sales, then the body of your letter will explain how. Let's say you operate a medical billing practice and you're writing a sales letter that you'll use to follow up telephone conversations with cold prospects, such as, say, group medical practices. And let's say you have asserted in your opening paragraph that you will help the medical practice become more profitable. The body of your letter should go on to explain how you will help the practice increase its cash on hand, reduce its uncollected payments, and free up staff time to perform more vital tasks.

Your final paragraph should contain a summary of the initial benefits. Then, depending upon your type of business and whether your sales letter makes any special offers, you may also include a "call to action" that helps increase responses to your literature. An independent manufacturer's rep selling industrial rubber flooring might include a call to action such as, "And when you place your order within the next 30 days you'll receive 10 percent off as a special thank you."

For most business-to-business sales, however, a closing paragraph is more likely to include a summary of your benefits and a description of the action you plan to take, such as, "I'll telephone you soon to discuss further the ways Acme Medical Billing can help increase the profitability of your group practice, thanks to increased cash flow and the reduction of uncollected payments from insurance companies." In the absence of a special offer, it's best to take responsibility for following up. State what you'll do and carry through on your promised action.

■ Rule #4: Don't Worry About Length

There's a popular misconception that sales letters must be kept to one page in length. One page is often preferred because recipients may tune out the longer they are asked to spend with your letter. A five- or six-page sales letter, for example, that accompanies a brochure or sell sheets and a whole package of literature, may be lightly scanned and set aside for future reading. This is risky, because you take a chance your prospect may never get back to your materials and miss out on several important facts buried on the fourth page. But if you follow the formula above and put the benefits in the first paragraph, explain features in the body copy, and close with a summary of your benefits and any special offer, you should feel free to take as much space as you need to tell a compelling story.

■ Rule # 5: Make It Easy to Read

Mail your professional correspondence on company stationery with matching envelopes. It's best to avoid cutesy stationery and artwork. This holds true for most businesses, with a few exceptions. For instance, if you're selling the services of a day-care center, stationery with a fun juvenile motif may work well for you. In most cases, though, your words should be powerful enough to carry the message without the need for stylized fonts, special graphics, or lots of boxes and arrows. Don't confuse a sales letter with standard direct mail (see chapter 14). Many of the bells and whistles used to attract readers who are unfamiliar with your company and its message via direct mail, are inappropriate for sales letters to prospects with whom you have met or spoken.

Choose clear, easy-to-read fonts, double-space your text, and include spaces between paragraphs. Use bullets to itemize facts, such as a list of special features. Just be careful not to overdo it. Of course, your choices will depend on the nature of your business. When a management consultant uses bullets, she or he should take a conservative approach. But if you're selling skateboards, you can let loose and have fun—maybe even use a clip art graphic of a skateboarder for your bullet points.

- **Rule #6: Incorporate a P.S.**

Did you know that the postscript is read almost immediately after the reader opens your letter? The reader will actually scan it long before the body copy. So for many types of sales letters, consider adding a P.S. that incorporates a brief reference to your benefit or special offer. If your P.S. piques the reader's interest, you have a better chance he or she will spend time with your letter.

To continue with the medical billing company example above, a postscript that refers to a special offer might say, "Did you know, group medical practices that rely on medical billing services can increase their profitability by 20 percent? Complete the profitability assessment enclosed and we'll show you how."

SAMPLE LETTERS

To illustrate the best way to create successful sales letters, and to have a little fun, I've created a fictitious company that I'll call PC Troubleshooters, Inc. Okay, you caught me. I made this business up for a good reason. I wish it existed nationwide because so many home business owners want and need this kind of service. Let's look at the features and benefits of this fictitious company, then read two sample sales letters. The first is written the wrong way, as an inner-directed self-promotional tool. The second is an example of a solid sales letter.

COMPANY OVERVIEW

- **Name:**
PC Troubleshooters, Inc.

- **Positioning statement:**
Your Information Services Team

- **Benefits:**
reduce downtime (due to computer problems)

gain peace of mind

save time (you don't have to learn technical computer operations)

save money

- **Features:**
service in your home or office

on call for emergencies

skilled in all major operating systems

rescue data from hard drive crashes

recommend and install system upgrades

diagnose software incompatibilities and glitches

install new software

bonded and insured

annual contracts available with low rates

annual contract upgrades include loaner PCs

small businesses don't need an information specialist on staff

- **Special offer:**
20 percent off your first service call.

- **The Wrong Way**
Read through the following example of how to write a weak sales letter. See how many problems you can spot. Assume you're reading a letter that has been sent to a prospect along with a company brochure following a telephone call.

Dear Sir:

PC Troubleshooters, Inc., is the service you've been looking for. After ten years' experience working with computers of all kinds, I founded this company to offer small and home-based business owners help with a range of computer challenges. No matter what your problem, we'll come to your home or office to solve it.

Some of the services we provide for businesses include installation of system upgrades and diagnosis of software incompatibilities and glitches, and we can often rescue data from hard drive crashes. My company's independent contractors are skilled in all major operating systems. Our clients report reduced downtime thanks to the way we keep their systems up and running, and increased peace of mind knowing that we're on call for emergencies.

You don't have to become a computer expert or hire an information systems staff member. Right now we're offering 20 percent off your first service call with an affordable service contract. If you're running a home-based business and depend daily on your PC, you'll be happy to know about our "PC on loan program," which keeps your business running even when your computer won't.

Call today to take advantage of this 20 percent discount offer and to learn more about how you can protect your business in the event of computer problems. I'm looking forward to hearing from you.

Sincerely,
John Jones

Here's a rundown of some of the more obvious problems with this letter.

The Salutation. Nothing reveals you're using a form letter more quickly than a generic Dear Sir or Dear Madam at the opening of your letter. This letter is a follow-up to a telephone conversation, but at first glance you'd never know it. If you want prospects to read your letters, always address them by name. And please take care to get the spelling right. You may have to contact a company's receptionist to confirm a spelling, but it's well worth the phone call.

Paragraph 1. The letter should begin by referring to the previous telephone conversation. If this prospect is like most, he receives numerous calls for products and services, and may not recall the conversation immediately upon receiving the letter. The most obvious problem with this paragraph is that it's inner-directed. It begins by addressing the writer's ten years' experience and his assertion that he can solve all the prospect's problems. The paragraph fails to use benefits to substantiate this claim and motivate the prospect to read on.

Paragraph 2. The features explained here would be more persuasive if they were combined with several others in a bulleted list. There's no need to mention that the company's services are delivered through a network of independent contractors unless this fact can help support a benefit, such as reduced costs or quicker response time in emergencies.

Paragraph 3. The special offer of 20 percent off is introduced here, which isn't necessarily a flaw. But the offer would attract more notice if it were first called to the prospect's attention in the P.S. (postscript) and referred to in this part of the body copy along with further information. Unfortunately, there isn't much additional info supplied here.

Paragraph 4. The writer expects the prospect to take action. This puts him in the position of sitting by the telephone waiting for it to ring.

Signature Block. There's no title following "John Jones." Even if he's the only employee, he should use the title of president, general manager, or even owner. It's not ego—it's accepted business practice—and lends professionalism and credibility to the letter.

▪ The Right Way

Dear Mr. Smith:

Thank you for taking time from your busy schedule to discuss your computer hardware and software challenges. For home businesses like yours that rely on a single PC, a simple computer problem can be a major headache when it results in downtime that causes you to lose business. PC Troubleshooters can prevent such losses by reducing your downtime during computer "emergencies," and provide the peace of mind that comes from knowing you have experts on call. We can even supply you with a PC until yours is up and running again.

How much time do you spend installing new software and correcting incompatibility problems? Are you frustrated with those time-wasting calls to technical support people who give you a few helpful tips and then leave you to muddle through alone? PC Troubleshooters can recommend and install system upgrades and a host of new software, plus provide step-by-step instruction on how to make them work for your business. And right now, to help you experience the many ways PC Troubleshooters can save you time and money, we're offering 20 percent off your first service call.

You'll get:

✓ On-call emergency service

✓ Service in the convenience of your own home office

✓ Technicians skilled in all major operating systems

✓ Repair and maintenance of your computer hard drive

✓ Quick diagnosis of software incompatibilities and glitches

✓ Comprehensive recommendations and installation of system upgrades

✓ Worry-free installation of new software

With PC Troubleshooters, you choose your level of support. Call us when there's an emergency or you'd like help with a particular challenge, such as installing new software and upgrading your system. Or sign up for an affordable annual contract that includes two service calls and membership in our PC Loaner Program. As a member you're guaranteed, should your system require off-site repair, you'll receive a quality machine on loan within twenty-four hours.

The enclosed brochure will give you more information about us. I'll telephone you soon to discuss further the many ways PC Troubleshooters can save you time and money, and ensure the peace of mind that comes from knowing you have an on-call information services team behind you.

Sincerely,

John Jones
President

P.S.: Don't forget, you'll save 20 percent off the cost of your in-home service. So whether you call for emergency help or want us to install a new system upgrade or software, you'll save on our already affordable rates.

The key to creating terrific sales letters is to focus on what the prospect "will get," not on what you offer. Make your letters outer-directed like the one above. This will keep the reader engaged and put you closer to reaching your sales goals.

CHECKLIST

✓ Decide what types of letters you'll need to fit the variety of sales requirements your company normally faces. How will they be used? Prepare to write a different version of your sales letter for varying uses, such as to accompany proposals or as a cover letter for your company brochure. Always match your message to the needs of the specific recipients.

✓ Schedule enough time to carefully craft each letter—no less than several hours each. Maintain your letters in a word processing program or contact manager. Some contact managers contain generic sample letters already prepared. Unfortunately, they are not always well crafted. Before using generic letters, review them to be sure they follow the guidelines in this chapter.

✓ Refer to the benefit statement you created after reading chapter 1, and modify it as necessary to fit the context of each letter. As you write your sales letters, be certain each introduces your company's chief benefits in the first paragraph, uses the body of the letter to communicate features, and restates the benefits along with your call to action in the closing paragraph.

✓ Scan the layout of your letters to be sure they're easy to read and free of unnecessary special fonts and graphics. Personalize every letter with the prospect's name and reference to any previous contact or relationship. The more you personalize your letters, the more likely they are to be read.

THIRTEEN

Make Meetings Count

Truth: To win more business, you must meet with the right prospects and master a unique set of skills.

■ ■ ■

Think back over the time before you started your home-based business, perhaps when you worked for a previous employer. During your career there, how many business meetings would you say you led? A hundred? Thousands? Now answer this: How many business meetings did you lead that were for the purpose of closing sales? Unless you're a sales and marketing professional, you probably haven't had much experience at it. And you're not alone. Home-based business owners often have many years' experience in their own fields before founding their businesses, but most don't start out with expertise in making sales.

Yet for a wide range of home-based businesses, your ability to meet with prospects and move them closer to a buying decision is a vital component of long-term success. People hire people, not companies, and they hire people they like. Meetings allow you to build relationships with prospects, more fully present the unique benefits of your product or service, and learn much more about your prospects than is possible by telephone or electronic communications.

Three components make for successful meetings—the right timing, meeting only with qualified prospects, and good interpersonal skills.

QUALIFY YOUR PROSPECTS

Many types of business prospects have particular times of year during which they're able to make purchases. For example, if your prospects' fiscal year starts September first and you approach them in June for a purchase which must be made right away, chances are they'll turn you down. Even if they want to buy your product, their budget for the current fiscal year will probably be depleted or carefully allocated and you'll have to wait until after September first for them to buy. As you qualify prospects by telephone, note which times of year they're authorized to make purchases, or if seasonality affects their buying decisions. Then you can decide whether the timing is right for a meeting to establish your relationship, or if it should be postponed until the prospect is prepared to make a buying decision.

When new business meetings with prospects go awry, the problem often has nothing to do with your timing or skills. Instead, you may be meeting with the *wrong* prospects. It's common for inexperienced entrepreneurs to mistake prospects with no objections for those who are well qualified.

How do you tell the difference? Suppose you've started a home-based technology company that works with associations and other membership organizations to transfer their membership lists onto CD ROM. You telephone an association prospect and he tells you, "Our association hasn't considered renting its list in the past though it's something we might consider for sometime in the future. But I have no budget set aside and I would have to get permission from the board to take that kind of action. If you can come by next Tuesday, I have some time and we can talk about it."

Should you meet with this person? Probably not. His group has not determined a need to sell its list. There's no budget available without a lengthy approval process, and you don't know whether or not the board is predisposed to change its mind and allocate funds. This meeting looks like a time waster. Remember I told you it may cost over a hundred dollars every time you leave your office to call on a prospect? When you meet with a less-than-qualified prospect, you might as well just write them a check and mail it out, because you will have wasted your time and money.

Qualified prospects meet three criteria: They have a need for your product or service, they can afford it, and they are willing to pay for it. Let's continue with the same example, and say you call another association. Here's what a good prospect sounds like: "We've been renting our list for several years now, though we haven't necessarily considered the financial advantages of putting it on CD ROM, and I'm not sure what benefits we would gain by doing so. Plus, I'm very busy right now and I'm not sure when we'd be able to get together."

Despite his objections, this is a highly qualified prospect. Since he's already renting his list, he does have a need to earn income from sales of his members' names. There's reason to believe he has a budget he can draw on because he is working with vendors (probably your competitors) to supply his list in other formats. That means he meets the first two criteria for a good prospect. As for meeting the third criterion—demonstrating a willingness to pay for your product—he may not be ready yet, but that's why you created your sales and marketing program. Someone who is working with your competition meets the three criteria for a good (think qualified!) prospect. They have a perceived need for what you offer, they have the budget, and they're willing to spend it.

MEETING ONE-ON-ONE

When it comes to the skills involved in handling face-to-face meetings with prospects, you may be better prepared than you think, since every interaction must focus on the benefits your prospects will derive by using your product or service.

- You developed a benefit statement after reading chapter 1.

- Your competitive analysis from chapter 2 helped you to position your company.

- You learned how to use open- and closed-end questions to uncover and fill needs in a friendly, noncombative, and supportive way in chapter 10.

Whether on the telephone or in person, it's vital to ask good questions and listen carefully to the answers whenever you're meeting with prospects. This will give you the necessary insight to propose reasonable solutions and demonstrate the benefits of using your product or service. Unlike a telephone conversation, however, a face-to-face meeting with a prospect, particularly when it takes place on their turf, offers you several helpful advantages.

■ Property Observations

When you visit a prospective customer or client's home or office, the environment itself will contain interesting information that will help you build rapport and the foundation for a positive relationship. Imagine you're visiting the office of a prospective client. You notice on one wall there's a print of a Warhol painting, and on the other are signed photographs of your prospective client with three famous golfers. Two golf trophies sit on the credenza behind the prospect's desk. Next to them is a radio cassette player on which you can hear a tape of the Beatles' *Sgt. Pepper* album playing softly. By noticing these things, you've made a series of helpful *property observations*. All of these items provide insight to your prospect's likes in art and music and his favorite hobby.

Let's say you're not much of a golf lover and you don't know anything about Warhol. But you can tell the prospect how much you enjoy the Beatles and relate an anecdote about a certain song or album. This will help you begin your relationship on common ground. What if you hate art, know nothing about golf, and are clueless about the Beatles? You still have an opportunity to build rapport by looking for other commonalities. Perhaps you're a football fan and have autographed photos from your favorite players. You can share stories of how you both came by your photos and the pride you have in displaying them. There's almost always a way to build a bridge if you look for it.

▪ Pay Attention to Body Language

Your second advantage when meeting in person versus by telephone is the opportunity to observe body language. You don't need to be a psychologist to pick up on information your prospect is sending you during a meeting. Is he sitting back with arms folded across his chest, or leaning forward, making eye contact with you and nodding his head? Pay careful attention to signals like these. A prospect who is leaning back in his chair with arms folded may be indicating that he's unconvinced, has withdrawn his participation, or is otherwise bored. It's your job to draw him out, using open-end questions in an attempt to reengage him in your discussion and uncover the objections that have given rise to his physical demonstration of resistance.

In a meeting, just like on a cold or warm call, your prospect should be doing most of the talking. If he's sitting back with arms folded, it may be because he feels he can't get a word in edgewise! In short, there may be any number of reasons for a prospect's physical behavior. So watch carefully to detect clues to his emotional state that you can use to guide your conversation.

▪ Use the Right Sales Tools

Effective use of the sales tools we discussed in chapter 5 can dramatically increase your chances for a successful meeting. Always use the highest quality tools, matched to the needs of your specific product or service and your audience. For example, a building contractor we'll call Lee specializes in adding sunrooms to residences. He's meeting with homeowners, a husband and wife, in their suburban living room. The only information the couple has about Lee is what they've gleaned from the postcard they responded to and from a conversation on the telephone prior to this meeting. Therefore, most of their impressions, favorable or not, will depend on this first face-to-face meeting.

They're positively reassured when Lee's vehicle has clear and attractive signage positioning his company as a specialist in sunroom additions. Lee presents his card at the door and is dressed in appropriate casual attire. During the meeting, he uses a presentation folder to share photographs of completed sunrooms. This helps the couple visualize the way they will use the new space and how it will enhance the value of their home. As he begins to close for the opportunity to supply an estimate, Lee presents a color brochure that shows his license number and states that his workers are bonded. The high-quality brochure also supports the image he has created for his firm. To close, Lee provides a list of references on company letterhead and an estimate on a preprinted form that he fills in as he reviews the job with the couple, who are now happily envisioning the completed work. After a follow-up call to discuss the estimate, Lee gets a verbal okay and he drops by with a contract on letterhead for their signature and a deposit.

Just this handful of sales tools, combined with Lee's professional demeanor, have played a crucial role in closing a high-ticket sale for his firm. Note that Lee carefully matched his presentation tools to his audience. He used a basic presentation folder with photographs to show the couple real examples of how their neighbors have enjoyed the benefits of his company's services.

Here's another example. A Web designer I'll call Gerry is meeting with several executives of a midsized business. To demonstrate his company's abilities, he has carefully selected his sales tools to match the high-tech business he's presenting. Gerry makes a PowerPoint presentation using an LCD projector and notebook computer to provide a company overview and demonstrate his capabilities. Then, with the assistance of a cordless modem, he uses the same technology to go directly to the Web and walks his prospects through the bells and whistles of several sites his company has designed. This thoroughly engages the participants, as they can see and experience firsthand the way Gerry's firm has created successful sites for a host of companies.

MAINTAIN A PROFESSIONAL IMAGE

Your personal style and demeanor will also have a positive or negative impact on the outcome of your meetings. As home-based business owners, we're fortunate to be able to dress and behave as we please in our own environments. But when we leave our home offices to call on prospects, we should match our attire, just as we do our presentation tools, to the dress requirements of our prospects' companies.

▪ When Meeting at Home
When meetings take place in your own home office, keep personal items and clutter to a minimum. If your home office serves a dual purpose, such as by doubling as a guest bedroom, it can be redecorated to put on a more professional face during business hours by replacing the bed with a sleep sofa and moving personal accessories, such as toiletries, out of sight. A number

of home-based business owners mentioned throughout this book have created showcases for their talents in their own homes. Architect Mark McInturff has created a separate building to house his practice, which is a part of his home and office compound. And interior designer Barbara Schlattman's glass-walled home office overlooks a golf course, and its built-in cabinetry is highly functional as well as a beautiful demonstration of her design abilities.

CHECKLIST

✓ Are you prequalifying your prospects by telephone prior to meeting with them? To increase the success from your important meetings, meet only with those who fit at least the first two of the three criteria for a good prospect: They have a perceived need for what you offer and can afford to buy it. Your job is to demonstrate the benefits they'll receive when they buy from *you*.

✓ In your next meeting, use your powers of observation to build rapport. Watch for physical clues to your prospect's state of mind to help guide your conversation.

✓ Choose quality sales tools that match the type of product or service you offer and make what you're selling "immediate and real" to your prospects.

FOURTEEN

Send Effective Direct Mail

Truth: Effective direct mail follows a precise creative formula.

■ ■ ■

Each day, your mailbox fills with of all sorts of direct mail. How do you decide which to open? How much time do you spend with an open piece of mail before you decide whether you're interested? Several seconds? Less? Believe it or not, the whole process—from when you first look at your mail to when you decide whether or not to throw away an open piece—usually takes eight seconds or less.

Direct mail marketing is one of American advertisers' most powerful tools. In 1999, U.S. businesses spent nearly $42 billion on it. And in the year 2003 the Direct Marketing Association predicts U.S. advertisers will spend $52.7 billion on direct mail in the United States alone.

Not to be confused with sales letters, which are used to follow up contacts with prospects, direct mail pieces are sent out by the thousands to qualified lists of recipients. Many home business owners are heavy users of direct mail, because it can help them reach their top prospect groups quickly and with less personal expenditure of time than contacting them on an individual basis. A positive response rate for a direct mail campaign averages about 1 or 2 percent and will vary based on the product, the offer, the price, and the quality of the list used. With so many important elements, direct mail marketing is rarely a do-it-yourself job. There are several distinct project phases, including list rental, creative development, printing, labeling, and mailing.

The truth is, there are some jobs you can handle on your own and others that you must trust to professionals. Finding the right list can be tricky business, but you can probably manage it yourself, perhaps with some input the first time around from a list broker. But you should not try to write your own copy and design the creative components yourself. Instead, work with a copy and design team, using the information provided here as a guide. You can ask your team to work directly with a printer on your behalf, or take delivery of your materials on disk and save some money by working directly with the printer yourself.

Qualified mailing houses are easy to find. They'll handle the labeling and mailing of your direct mail campaign for you. To simplify your life further, you may want to work with a company that also handles printing. This will save you the time you'd otherwise spend developing a relationship and working one-on-one with a single vendor for printing alone.

DIRECT MAIL LISTS

There are at least four types of lists available for rent.

• Many publications rent their subscriber lists. If you're only interested in names and addresses, publications with paid circulations may fit your needs. Publications with non-paid, qualified circulation lists will generally have more in-depth information concerning their readers, such as their SIC codes and job titles. That means you'll be able to pick and choose just the readers you want to reach with your direct marketing campaign.

• Associations and other membership groups often make their lists available. They are excellent resources if you want to reach a group of people with a particular interest in common. Since most association and club memberships require payment of dues or other fees, you can be assured that the members on the list have a vested interest in that specific topic or issue, whether it's bicycling or gun regulation.

• Some of the very best lists contain names of people who have inquired about or purchased a product via direct mail in the past. If you're selling custom-made children's clothing, for example, a list of people who have recently purchased quality children's toys by mail might be of special use for you.

• Compiled lists are the least reliable, and often the least expensive as well. These are made up of names from directories such as the Yellow Pages, and the information may or may not have been verified. If you choose to purchase a compiled list, be certain there are guarantees in place to ensure its accuracy.

▪ List Formats
Your list will be supplied on pressure sensitive (peel and stick) or Cheshire labels, which must be applied professionally by machine at your mailing house. If you're purchasing more than one list to reach the same target audience, have them supplied in an electronic format so that your mailing house can do a merge/purge to eliminate duplicate names. Otherwise, those who re-

ceive more than one identical piece will be annoyed with you and you'll have wasted funds that could be used elsewhere.

To find the right list for your company, start at the reference department of a major public library. There, you'll find a Standard Rate and Data Service directory called the *Direct Marketing List Source* that includes most of the lists available in the United States divided by category. Review the listings and then contact the list vendors whose descriptions most closely match your requirements. The *Direct Marketing List Source* is a large directory that's also sold by subscription for approximately five hundred dollars a year including online access at www.srds.com. But if you plan a limited number of mailings per year or will use the same list vendors to reach a similar target audience time and again, you can avoid the subscription fees by working at the library with this important reference tool. At this writing, a Web site provided by Oxbridge Communications, Inc., www.mediafinder.com, is a free online resource. You can browse its mailing list directory by subject and use it much in the same way you would the SRDS.

▪ List Costs and Considerations

The base cost for list rental is expressed in cost per thousands (CPM). That, of course, is the cost to rent one thousand names, although most list vendors require a minimum purchase of five thousand names or a base fee. List costs rise when you add what are called "selections." These are charges for any special qualifying criteria you choose. Let's say you want to rent a list of consumers in specific zip codes. When you add selections, such as those who own their homes, have been in residence five years or more, and have two or more children in the household, your list costs will increase incrementally.

When making your list purchase, consider three additional factors. First, does the list vendor guarantee its list to be at least 94 percent deliverable? Quality vendors who have faith in their lists will offer guarantees and stand behind them. Should your list turn out to contain 10 percent undeliverable pieces due to address or other problems as a result of the list information, the actual reparation may be minimal. However, you're less likely to encounter difficulties when you work with a vendor who offers an up-front guarantee that its list is clean and deliverable.

The second important factor is how recently the list you plan to rent has been *cleaned*. Mailing information that is more than three months old may be outdated, resulting in a higher percentage of returned pieces.

Your third consideration is how often you'll be mailing to the same list. Studies often show that responses increase when you mail to the same list several times in a row. So if you plan to mail more than once within a three-month period, it pays to purchase a duplicate set of labels along with your first. This will be significantly less expensive than placing the same list order twice.

▪ Test Your Cost per Response

Overall, the most important factor to consider isn't your cost per thousand, it's your *cost per response*. That's why testing is vital if you wish to have a successful direct mail campaign over an extended period. Five thousand names is considered a typical quantity for a basic test. In addition to testing the list, you can test your offer, your product modifications, and your marketing pieces themselves. But test them one at a time, or you won't be able to tell which factor made the difference.

▪ Use a List Broker

If all of this sounds a little complicated, consider employing a list broker to purchase your list. These individuals or companies are compensated by commission from the list vendors, though they may also charge you an additional minimum fee. But their fee may be well worth it if they save you time and point you toward a list you might not have found on your own. The *Direct Marketing List Source* contains the names of list brokers, and you can also find them in the telephone directories of most major cities.

▪ Build Your Own List

Carol Hearty used to sell her unique, high-end ladies' bags wholesale to retailers, but when the economy changed in the late eighties, she says many shops that carried her work went under. After evaluating the market, Hearty decided to design products just for the upscale, juried retail craft shows. Now she's one of the most celebrated artists at many of the top shows, including the prestigious Smithsonian craft show and the American Craft Council shows in Baltimore, San Francisco, and Philadelphia—often more than twenty shows a year. She applies for only those shows whose attendees match her target audience profile: upscale female consumers who are interested in unique, creative designs and are willing to pay one hundred dollars or more for a bag that might resemble a tornado sculpted in leather or for a polished gourd with exquisite fittings.

She has built up a following thanks to her use of direct mail and her one-on-one relationships with customers—she will customize a design in the customer's choice of colors and make on-the-spot suggestions. Customers, and those who've signed up to be on her mailing list at the shows, receive notices of upcoming shows in their area. This direct mail helps ensure her customers keep coming back, and results in repeat sales.

DIRECT MAIL COMPONENTS

Just as you must narrowly focus on a painstakingly selected target audience in order to buy (or create) the best possible list, you must carefully craft your creative materials in order to produce the desired result. While your direct mail campaign can be composed of simple postcards, most direct mail packages contain five components: a carrier envelope, a cover letter, an order form, optional inserts, and a return envelope. You can add more pieces as long as each one explains an additional benefit. When working with your creative copy and design team, be sure they resist the temptation to overdesign. Keep the materials simple, although you'll want to avoid a monochromatic package. Your carrier envelope and your letter stock may be consistent, but use different textures, colors, or even sizes for your other pieces to avoid a boring, lackluster presentation.

▪ The Carrier Envelope

The look of the envelope itself can make or break your campaign. Not only is it your carrier but it can determine whether or not your recipient opens and spends time with your package. Your envelope is your handshake—so make it as personal and specific to the needs of your prospects as possible. Avoid labels that are addressed to "occupant" or "current resident" and instead address each recipient by name. Include a teaser on your envelope. This is a simple line that must grab the recipients' attention and incite them to open the materials and read on.

▪ Your Cover Letter and Order Form

Once the package is opened, the cover letter is the most important of all the components. It should contain a *Johnson box*—the sentence or headline before the salutation that will highlight your marketing hook or offer. Following your salutation, which should address the recipient by name if possible, a good opener will establish rapport with the reader and pique his or her interest. Be prepared to supply your copywriter with your benefit statement and list of important features. Then help the writer determine what the single focus of your piece will be so that he or she can lead the package with it. What will have the greatest appeal to your target audience? Will it be your special offer or your product, for example? Direct mail copywriting is challenging work that requires skill and practice to perfect. A professional copywriter with experience in direct mail will use benefits in the opener, explain them with features in the body copy, weave in your special offer, and include a P.S.

Since the P.S. is the second thing people read when they open your letter, it should contain some aspect of the offer. Once your Johnson box and P.S. interest them, your readers will review the body copy. Not before.

The order form may be a part of your cover letter or a separate piece. Above all, make it clear, brief, and easy to fill out. Include a fax number on your order form. And always put a telephone number (preferably toll-free) on every page in your package.

▪ Odd Sizes and Formats

Don't be surprised if your creative team suggests you do an odd-size package. This will help it stand out in the mail, and packages that get noticed may be more likely to be opened. The cost to produce larger pieces may be nominal, particularly if your list is small.

Dimensional Mailers. When mailing to an extremely small, well-qualified list of top prospects, you may want to consider using dimensional mailers. This term applies to pieces that are mailed in boxes or tubes. Think about it. Could you receive a nicely wrapped box in the mail and not open it?

The component parts of a dimensional mailing package differ from those of a standard direct mailer. Typically, the box will contain a novelty item and a card or letter with minimal copy. Suppose you owned a travel agency and you were promoting weekend getaways to your best executive clients. You might send "a mini vacation kit in a box," such as a pair of sunglasses and a miniature umbrella and deck chair accompanied by a letter promoting exciting, short-stay getaways to exotic locations.

Direct mail can be a dynamic tool for your home-based business. Before embarking on your first campaign, assemble a qualified team including a copywriter and designer for creative development and a vendor or vendors that can handle printing, mailing, and labeling. Then shop extensively for your list, either on your own or with the help of a list broker, and follow the rules in this chapter to develop a package with the right components and content. Luckily, direct mail has a precise formula and experts abound who can assist you in getting it right the first time and every time.

CHECKLIST

✓ Review your target audience profile. When you've made it as narrow as possible, you can begin your list search. Start at the public library with the *Direct Marketing List Source*, or use online or other resources to find a list that most narrowly matches your target audience profile.

✓ Discuss your selections (qualifying criteria) with the list vendors to narrowly focus on only your best prospects. Shop for the most favorable cost per thousand on a guaranteed list that has been recently cleaned.

✓ Assemble your team of vendors. Carefully interview copy and design professionals by reviewing their portfolios. Always select a team that has experience in direct mail. Other forms of copy and design differ significantly, and your design and copy team must understand the lengthy list of requirements for an effective direct mail package. Interview printers and mailing houses to look for your best fit. Bear in mind, you may have to choose direct mail specialists from outside your own market area in order to find those with the most desirable rates and capabilities. Trade magazines and journals that publish lists of direct mail vendors and the Direct Marketing Association (212-

768-7277) are excellent resources for locating honest, qualified vendors.

✓ Work with your creative team to be certain your package contains all five important components. Clearly communicate your company's benefits and features to the team and be prepared to work with them to develop a special offer that will increase the response rates for your campaign.

FIFTEEN

Make Smart Advertising Buys

Truth: Successful advertising depends on choosing the right media, creating an appealing message, and buying frequent exposure.

■ ■ ■

Which would you prefer: to reach one thousand qualified prospects all at once or speak to them individually over time? Reaching a thousand prospects at once would save you considerable time and increase your customer or client base much faster, giving you access to increased capital for expanding your business or pure profit. Certainly that's appealing. But if you knew you'd have to run an ad campaign to reach those one thousand top prospects at once, would the idea sound less enticing to you? If you're among the many home-based business owners who shy away from advertising due to uncertainties about how you can make it work for your business, you may be missing out on opportunities to increase your income.

For many home-based business owners, placing advertising, like sales and marketing in general, is a foreign and somewhat frightening concept. American companies spend billions of dollars a year on advertising, and thanks to every conceivable type of study over the past several decades, there is no doubt—when done properly—advertising does work. For some home business owners in certain professions, print and broadcast advertising are inappropriate avenues for reaching their target audiences. And if that's the case for your business, you should spend more time reading the chapters about direct mail marketing (chapter 14), public relations (chapter 17), and the upcoming chapter on out-of-home advertising for information on place-based media (chapter 16). But for most types of businesses, print and broadcast advertising are tried and true means of communicating a message to prospect groups.

Advertising production is not a do-it-yourself job, so you'll definitely want to put your work in expert hands. Traditional advertising agencies are compensated in two ways: by charging for creative production and by taking 15 percent commission on the media they place on your behalf. For that reason, the smaller your advertising campaign (and budget!) the less successful you're likely to be in finding a large, full-service agency to create and place your campaign. Instead, most home business owners use small design firms or independent teams consisting of a copywriter and art director with experience creating the type of advertising that's called for. If you decide to work in this fashion, you'll hire a team to create your materials and handle the placement yourself.

PRINT MEDIA BUYS

To plan a print media buy, use the Standard Rate and Data Service (SRDS) directories at a major library as I described in chapter 14, on target marketing. There are separate directories for business and consumer magazines and newspapers, and weekly/community newspapers. Contact each of the media outlets to obtain media kits and sample publications. Then follow the following three steps for choosing the right media.

▪ Step 1: Keep Waste Circulation to a Minimum

Review the readership information in each of the media kits from the publications you're evaluating. Select those that most closely match the demographics of your target audience with the least amount of waste. For example, let's say there's a horticulturist named Mark who specializes in incorporating water features into urban landscape designs. Suppose Mark lives in Gaithersburg, Maryland, which is a suburb of Washington, D.C., about a half hour's drive from the city. Should he place his advertising in his free local newspaper, the *Gaithersburg Gazette*, or in the *Washington Post* with its huge circulation? While the *Post* has tens of thousands of readers who live in apartments, or don't fit Mark's target audience profile for age and income, still his client base comes from the entire metro area and he may have to put up with (and pay for) the waste circulation—the papers that go to readers who do not fit the demographics of his primary target audience.

Now let's suppose a woman named Rita also lives in Gaithersburg and makes custom maternity dresses. Unlike Mark, her business comes predominantly from the local Gaithersburg area, since typical customers for this type of service aren't willing to drive long distances. So, when using only this criterion, the *Washington Post* presents too much wasted circulation, and the most efficient buy for Rita appears to be her local paper, the *Gaithersburg Gazette*.

▪ Step 2: Choose Media Your Prospects Consult for Information on Your Type of Product or Service

Let's say you've examined the readership of a publication and found it includes a desirable percentage of your target audience, along with an acceptable amount of waste. But what if there's no editorial or competitive advertising in your product or service category? You may have to select another publication instead.

In recent years, print media has become increasingly specialized. You'll find a magazine for virtually every type of reader or special interest. And newspapers, too, have followed suit, with sections dedicated to carrying a different kind of information each day. In the Monday Business section, for example, you might find financial advertising and editorial. On Wednesday, the Food section may be devoted to specials and recipes. Like directories such as the Yellow Pages, these special newspaper sections become "search corridors." That's where readers look when they've made a decision to buy. If a publication you're evaluating has few or no competitive ads or editorial that relate to what you're marketing, then it's not a search corridor for your type of product or service, and buyers are looking elsewhere for information.

So after Rita confirms that her free local newspaper reaches her target audience with the least amount of waste, she also has to determine if there is a section that regularly devotes space to advertising or editorial featuring women's apparel. If so, the publication meets the first two of three vital selection criteria. However, there must also be proof that the newspaper is not just *received* by her target audience—it must also be *read*.

You see, your prospects have to value the medium you're considering. Paid and controlled circulation publications tend to have interested, involved readers. But a free newspaper gets tossed on your lawn whether you have any interest in it or not. Before running your advertising in this type of environment, ask the ad sales staff to provide you with stories of advertisers who have succeeded through using their newspaper, or for third-party research documenting what percentage of the paper's recipients read three out of four issues.

▪ Step 3: Plan for Sufficient Frequency

Once you have narrowed your selection down to a handful of publications, choose the ones in which you can afford to advertise with enough frequency to ensure penetration of your message. You may be surprised to learn that the term *frequency* doesn't refer to the number of times you run your ad. It's the number of times readers can be expected to see it. The formula for determining frequency that advertising professionals use varies based on the type of publication—whether it's a trade or consumer magazine or newspaper, for example.

Frequency Rates. Let's say you're a software inventor and you run a full-page ad in *PC World*. You won't have a frequency of one. Instead, you'll have a frequency of about 0.40 to 0.85. That means that about 40 to 85 percent of that publication's readers can be expected to see your full-page ad in that issue. This accounts for why you'll typically see the same ad or ad series run six or more times in consecutive issues of a magazine, and thirteen or more times in a row in your favorite newspaper.

One exposure to an ad message is rarely effective, except for buyers with the most acute need. It will generally take several exposures to your message to stimulate a reader to action over the course of your sales cycle. The more complex your message, the more frequency it requires. For home business owners whose places of business can't readily be visited by consumers, advertising represents a virtual storefront. When you advertise, your store is "open." And the out-of-sight, out-of-mind syndrome truly applies in advertising. An ongoing presence in a particular publication can help build a comfort level in the minds of prospects. It connotes stability, profitability, substance, and experience.

▪ Estimate Costs

The final step for making your media selections is to realistically evaluate the cost to advertise consistently over time in each publication you choose. For Mark to run a quarter-page black-and-white ad in the weekly Home section of the *Washington Post* would cost approximately $3,100 or more. To achieve some frequency, twelve insertions would cost over $37,000. Based on this pricing information, our fictitious horticulturist, Mark, might decide to place his advertising schedule with the paper. On the other hand, he might believe the cost would take too big a bite out of his budget, especially with the extent of the waste circulation, and choose another newspaper or area magazine in which he could afford to advertise with enough frequency to achieve his goals. He could also use additional marketing tactics to complement his advertising schedule, as described in chapter 21. Mark might work with retail plant nurseries throughout the metro area to set up water garden displays with discreet signage to direct shoppers to his firm. He could use public relations targeting key media, and he might set up a special referral program that paid finders' fees to members of the landscape trade who sent clients his way.

BROADCAST ADVERTISING

With the proliferation of cable TV channels and the new affordability of television advertising thanks to local cable systems, more small business owners are using television advertising than ever. If you plan to make a national, regional, or market-by-market broadcast buy, your budget will probably be sufficient to hire a qualified advertising agency to handle production and placement for you. But if you want to place your campaign on local cable, you may be able to work directly with a cable representative to set up the best schedule to reach your primary target audience. They should also recommend a production company that regularly works with their "direct" clients.

One note of caution: Nothing can torpedo your campaign faster than a low-end, poorly produced television spot. American TV viewers are accustomed to the high-quality spots run by national advertisers with multimillion-dollar budgets. You don't have to outspend Pepsi, but if your budget forces you to cut corners on basic production values, it will be immediately apparent on the screen. It's best to choose another, less-costly medium than to air spots that stand out for all the wrong reasons.

In smaller media markets, radio can be a terrific way to communicate with your target audience due to the affordability of the average spot. To help your spots stand out from the crowd, consider radio sponsorships. Opening billboards can help build name awareness and frequency for your tagline, and guarantee your spot will be positioned first at the beginning of the commercial break. That's helpful because no one really knows how many listeners have hit another station button by the time the fourth spot in a row comes on.

When buying broadcast time, beware of any radio, TV, or cable company rep that offers you an affordable buy featuring a large number of spots unless the rep can demonstrate to you that the times at which the spots will run, or the programs during which they'll air, are those that will best reach your specific target group. There's a good chance a lot of those cheap spots will be "ROS," which stands for "run of station," and end up airing during the middle of the night or early Sunday morning, when there are the fewest listeners or viewers. In broadcast, it's not the *number* of spots you run, it's who sees or hears them that matters. That's why advertisers like McDonald's are willing to pay millions for one spot during the Super Bowl. The least expensive spots sold are those that air during the hours and programs that have the fewest listeners or viewers.

EVALUATE YOUR RESULTS

What if you have what you think are terrific ads or spots, and they're simply not working? The most terrific ads in the world won't pull if the right people don't see them and feel compelled to act "now," or when they do respond there are problems in follow-through. Good ads sometimes fail when they run in the wrong place or at the wrong time.

▪ Check Your Placement

Suppose you opened a sporting goods store a mile away from the neighborhood mall. True, your rent would be lower, but you'd have less traffic than the stores in the mall and, consequently, fewer sales. The same thing happens when you place your print ad outside of a search corridor. If all the advertising for your type of product or service runs in the newspaper on Wednesday, but your ad appears in the same section on Thursday, you will have effectively taken your company out of the running in the same way as if you were selling cereal and you removed all of your product from the store shelves during the busiest shopping hours. Always review the publications and broadcast media in which you plan to advertise and decide when and where your ads should run.

▪ Test Your Offer

Sometimes a perfectly good ad is bogged down by a weak or ineffective offer. Examine all your competitors' offers and then develop one that you believe will motivate your prospects to take immediate action. If possible, test your offer in informal focus groups—roundtable discussions among friends or others who are members of your target audience. If one offer doesn't pull after several insertions, strengthen it or change it altogether until you find one that pulls. Then, when responses to that successful offer begin to decline, it will be time to change it again.

▪ Remove Sales Barriers

If your terrific ad isn't pulling, there may be sales barriers preventing your prospects from taking advantage of your offer. For example, failure to include a toll-free number for those outside your immediate market area puts up an instant sales barrier because prospects hesitate to take even a small financial risk to investigate an unknown. Callers who reach a busy signal or an unprofessional-sounding message are also being thwarted by sales barriers. In both cases, voicemail from your local telephone company, or a multiline telephone with multiple mailboxes, may be the answer (more in chapter 23).

You will also deter prospects if there are too many steps in your sales process. Imagine that a prospect who sees your ad in the local newspaper contacts you by telephone. You have a terrific conversation and promise to send the prospect additional literature. A week later, the prospect receives your literature in the mail. It includes a brochure and a letter that asks the prospect to call when he's ready to set up an appointment. This is an extremely motivated prospect and, undeterred, he decides to give you a call. Unfortunately, he encounters voicemail or your answering machine. You return his call within twenty-four hours, but miss him. Even such an enthusiastic prospect will lose interest when the selling process is so protracted. Walk through every action step in your sales process as if you were a prospective customer or client. Look for any opportunity to remove steps and sales barriers that lengthen the sales cycle or delay your ability to close.

If you're placing your own media without the assistance of an advertising agency or media buying service, you can use your contact management software to track the "materials closing" dates. These are the dates on which your creative art is due at each publication. You'll also need to provide your creative team with the exact production specifications required by each publication. This is easily found in the media kits or by contacting your reps.

In all, when you follow the three steps for effective media placement and carefully review the environment in which your advertising will run, you'll make educated and informed buys. And you'll stimulate responses from qualified prospects over time.

CHECKLIST

✓ Interview and hire a creative team that's experienced in producing advertising for the media you choose. Review their portfolios and look at how they've created materials for similar products. A copywriter who regularly writes retail ads for stores may have a hard time writing high-tech ads for trade journals, for example. If you're in the refrigeration business, you don't need to locate a team that knows as much about refrigeration as you do. What you want are professionals who, by virtue of their experience marketing similar products, can speak the language your target audience is accustomed to seeing (or hearing) in the media you're using.

✓ Use reference tools, such as the SRDS directories, to research the media that reach your target audience. Contact print media for their media kits.

✓ Choose publications that reach your unique target audience with a minimal amount of waste, are read for information on what you offer, and in which you can afford to advertise frequently over time.

✓ Beware of any broadcast outlet that offers you an inexpensive schedule that includes many ROS spots. A good schedule will include those programs or dayparts (the times of day) that attract the largest number of listeners or viewers.

✓ Examine all the steps in your sales process and remove any barriers that may be reducing your lead or conversion rates.

SIXTEEN

Use Place-Based Advertising

Truth: New media let you market where your customers are.

■ ■ ■

What if there were no rules about when and how often you could put your message in front of your prospective clients or customers? No matter where they went during their waking hours, you could reach them. Sound impossible? Well, welcome to America, where we're exposed to thousands of marketing messages daily in some of the most unlikely and unexpected ways.

In the last two chapters, I've discussed direct mail, print advertising in newspapers and magazines, and a bit about broadcast, including radio and television. But these traditional advertising methods are just the tip of the iceberg. Over the past decade or more, televison audiences became increasingly fragmented due to the proliferation of cable options. The rising cost of advertising in broad-based print media, and the ability to create unique magazines and other print options for virtually every special interest under the sun, also contributed to the fragmentation of media audiences. Major media companies and advertisers responded to this change in the advertising environment by creating a plethora of new communication tools that went out and found the customer wherever he or she happened to be.

Traditional out-of-home advertising—billboards, bus and bus shelter signs, subway dioramas and posters, and the like—were joined by the new media that also moved out of the home. The new marketing vehicles took on the name "place-based media" because the sites themselves draw the audience to the advertising. Now there are television screens in convenience stores, airports, and malls, posters in restaurants and nightclubs, special magazines in medical waiting rooms, and signage on taxi-tops, truck-mounted mobile billboards, and airplane banners. Even ads on movie screens have become commonplace. The new media, no longer content to go into homes via television, radio, magazines, newspapers, and direct mail, let you sell where your customers are, and reach them in an environment in which they'll be likely to think about and remember your message.

FISH WHERE THE FISH ARE

There are several categories of place-based media. Each category is based on the type of site where the media are found. Some sites target consumers where products can be purchased, such as stadium advertising for beer or movie-theater ads for popcorn and candy. The posters and racks of booklets found in veterinary waiting rooms are an interesting example of using place-based media at sites that lend credibility. Millions of Americans own pets, and at one time or another we can be found at the vet's office, whether for simple checkups and vaccinations or to have our four-legged loved ones treated for serious illnesses. While waiting, we read the pamphlets on the importance of heartworm testing, dental care, and a host of other topics that will help us care for our pets—all supported by the makers of pharmaceutical, flea-control, and pet supply products. These manufacturers are fishing where the fish are. They're talking to pet owners through media that will be of special interest to us in an environment in which we'll be more likely to read and remember the information. We may even take booklets home to refer to later or share with family members.

▪ Choose the Right Environment

Place-based media often make use of sites that offer environmental stimulation, such as soup advertising on ski lifts. This form of place-based advertising helps you reach your prospects where and when they're likely to be receptive. Video monitors in health clubs, for example, allow advertisers to reach audiences at a time when they're health and body-image conscious. After a half-hour on a stair climber, wouldn't you be more interested in watching information on a new, healthy drink? Would you be just as receptive if you saw the drink advertised in your morning newspaper while at the breakfast table eating eggs with bacon and a muffin? Probably not. In this case, the site reaches people who are concerned about their health and are working hard to get in shape. Messages for products that help them achieve that goal will be better received in that environment.

Remember our horticulturist from the last chapter, Mark, who created his own place-based media by cooperating with independently owned nurseries throughout his city. He set up water garden displays, using their materials and his talents, in exchange for signage with his company name, positioning statement, and telephone number. The plant nursery and garden center shoppers who see his displays are more prone to purchase the plants, tubs, or liners, and many will also contact Mark for his expertise in designing unique water features. They're prepared to consider what he has to offer because it's presented in the right environment.

▪ Put Your Message on Wheels

Other place-based media deliver high audience reach. Some years ago in New York City, Neal Weed and his partner created the first truck-mounted billboards for use in urban areas. Today, Neal Weed's son is the owner of Anytime Anywhere Outdoor, a mobile billboard company that transports signage through city streets on narrow, eye-catching trucks. The company has trucks stationed in New York, Chicago, and Los Angeles that they dispatch to cities throughout the United States. So if you want to send a message to clothing manufacturers and workers, you can have your truck-mounted billboard travel a predetermined route through New York's garment district during the hours it's most likely to be seen by the largest number of people in the "rag" trade.

▪ Reach a Captive Audience

Major media companies, too, recognizing the opportunity to help advertisers selectively target difficult-to-reach audiences, have created another category of place-based advertising media in new locations. Turner Private Networks, Inc., for example, has created the CNN Airport Network to reach the upscale Americans who frequent major airports. There are also TV screens in major shopping malls, and local entrepreneurs nationwide can now put their advertising messages on the big screen. National Cinema Network (NCN) has more than ten thousand movie screens under contract nationwide and, according to a company representative, each year they reach five times the number of people who would attend all professional baseball, football, basketball, and hockey games combined. If you don't need to reach NCN's full audience—54 million young adults ages eighteen to forty-nine every month—local advertisers can choose the theaters they want to use and their level of participation. People filing into movie theaters, like those waiting in line at theme parks, provide a place-based media opportunity to reach a captive, waiting audience.

▪ A Lower-Cost Opportunity

With so many out-of-home advertising methods from which to choose, there's an affordable way to reach your audience no matter what kind of product or service you market. A single, traditional one-third–page newspaper ad in a major market such as Los Angeles, Boston, Chicago, or New York may cost as much as several thousand dollars or more, while place-based media and other out-of-home advertising can help you reduce your marketing costs and create a campaign even if you're bootstrapping your home business start-up. For example, you could spend three thousand dollars to run an ad in the citywide newspaper on a single day, or you could display your message three times before every movie for a full week on all eight screens at your local cineplex for about three hundred dollars. Or for about one thousand dollars a month, less than the cost of one print ad on a single day, you could put your message on a bus shelter located at a key intersection.

Successful out-of home advertising typically requires a simple message. Mobile billboards and slides on a movie screen—even messages on supermarket clocks—must be simple. You wouldn't use these venues to explain a new invention, for example. So if you have a complex story to tell, look for place-based media that allow you to communicate in a brochure or video format. The point is to think creatively. No matter what you're marketing, chances are there's an out-of-home creative strategy that will fit within your budget and reach your best prospects in an environment that makes them receptive to your unique message. National Cinema Networks, for example, claims a high Nielsen-measured recall rate of more than 60 percent for local advertisers' messages.

TIPS FOR CHOOSING PLACE-BASED MEDIA

There are four points to consider when evaluating place-based media options.

The Cost Must Be Reasonable. You shouldn't have to pay for development of new technology or an emerging medium. Choose established media opportunities, or develop your own in cooperation with a vendor, the way the horticulturist above developed place-based promotions with the garden centers. In other words, if the place-based media opportunity requires ongoing video, you shouldn't be expected to purchase the video monitors and equipment, just to develop your programming and deliver it in a format to meet the requirements of the media outlet.

The Medium Must Fit the Environment. Think about the way your audience will experience delivery of your message. Will the environment be noisy, dark, excessively bright, or congested? The medium you use to communicate should be developed to fit the environment and the immediate needs of the target audience while they spend time there. For example, the horticulturist specializing in water features could have put a continuously running video that depicted him designing and assembling a water feature in the nurseries and garden centers. But it would have been more expensive and less appealing to his target audience than a beautiful and unique fountain with blooming water lilies. Plus, in a busy garden center, customers are walking back and forth carrying plants and wheeling carts. Video is better suited to a seated, captive audience.

The Medium Should Be Easily Accessible and User-Friendly. What's the best reason to put your company name or slogan on a supermarket clock? Everyone who visits the supermarket can easily see and read it, of course. The same holds true for wallboards in your dentist's waiting room and the racks of brochures at the veterinary clinic. Place-based media excel at making your message stand out from the crowd. Traditional media often have cluttered environments—many magazines have multiple ads on every page and the growing number of spots per television program has created a nation of remote control "zappers." Typically, place-based media offer less advertising clutter in a more consumer-friendly environment.

The Environment Must Be Compatible with Your Message. A business consultant, for example, wouldn't use movie theater advertising, even though his or her target audience might consist of adults under forty-nine, because the message wouldn't be compatible with the entertainment orientation of the site.

To find an out-of-home advertising medium to fit the needs of your home-based business, start at a major public library with an SRDS directory called the *Out-of-Home Advertising Source.* This is a unique directory that breaks down out-of-home advertising by type. You'll find companies that help you place advertising in shopping malls and movie theaters, on transit systems, in airports, and in high schools and colleges. If your home business makes custom surfboards, you can even locate a company to fly an aerial banner up and down the busiest beaches in your area. And if you can't find an established place-based advertising medium that lets you sell where your best customers are, you can always create one!

CHECKLIST

✓ Make a list of the out-of-home locations your best customers frequent. In which of these locations are they most likely to think about your type of product or service?

✓ Visit these locations—supermarkets, movie theaters, theme parks, medical offices, and so on—to see which place-based media are in use there. Use the SRDS to look for companies that offer standard advertising contracts to place your media in these out-of-home sites.

✓ Test an out-of-home opportunity with a short-term commitment. Evaluate the results and, if positive, incorporate this marketing strategy into your annual program.

SEVENTEEN

Establish a Public Relations Program

Truth: Public relations is "free" publicity you may get after months of work.

■ ■ ■

Remember Mark McInturff? He's the nationally recognized architect I told you about in chapter 8 whose home office, with five on staff, is in a separate building next to his home in a wooded compound in Bethesda, Maryland. In fact, it was an article in *Metropolitan Home* magazine featuring McInturff's home that led to an on-camera tour on the televison show, *Good Morning America*, followed by several other television tours and interviews.

Sounds like a wonderful run of luck, doesn't it? The truth is, luck had little to do with this public relations success. For the past twelve years, McInturff Architects has had a comprehensive public relations program in place, which has played an instrumental role in the growth of the practice.

AN EFFECTIVE PR CAMPAIGN

Let's look at the tactics employed in a classic public relations program that focuses on media placement. It involves four action steps, discussed below.

■ Step 1: Tell the Right Story

First, decide if what you have to say is new or noteworthy. The print and broadcast media are solely interested in stories that will be of unique interest to their readers, viewers, or listeners; help them sell more newspapers or magazines; or increase their ratings. So the information you develop for releases and stories must help them do one or both. McInturff Architects follows the trends in its industry. Ranch-style homes are a predominant architectural style in many parts of America, and as homeowners seek to renovate and update them, stories about the remodels are making news. In response to the heightened interest in this type of project, McInturff offered a story on a renovated ranch house that showcased his firm's talents.

Some business owners make the mistake of sending a steady stream of so-so information to the media in the hope that something will get picked up. This is an error because the recipients soon tune out (and discard) all their releases without giving them due review. It's best to wait until you have a story or news hook that is of real interest to the media and send out fewer releases overall.

■ Step 2: Match the Media to the Message

You must target the right media for your specific type of message. McInturff Architects has identified three types of magazines that it targets with varying messages:

• Shelter publications, including *Home*, *Metropolitan Home*, and *Architectural Digest*

- Professional media, including *Architectural Record* and *Architecture*

- Trade publications, including *Builder, Custom Home*, and *Residential Architect*

The firm's primary focus, according to Mark McInturff, is on the shelter magazines, because those reach its prospective clients. He says one placement in a shelter magazine gives seventy to one hundred thousand people the opportunity to look at his firm's work and call about doing a project of their own. Articles concerning awards McInturff Architects has won, or featuring completed projects, may also run in the professional and trade pubs. This builds referrals from other qualified professionals.

What types of media do your prospects look to for information about your type of product or service? Develop a targeted media list in much the same way you put together your advertising schedule. Use tools, such as the SRDS directories, to locate media your target audience look to for information about what you offer. If your focus is on print media, contact each publication to obtain sample issues and editorial calendars. Some major media outlets receive thousands of press releases *every day*, so direct your releases to a specific editor, journalist, or news director. Online sources can be extremely helpful when searching for the names to complete your list. Visit Media Finder, www.mediafinder.com, by Oxbridge Communications, Inc., for contact names, addresses, and telephone numbers.

Use a Contact Management System. Put your public relations lists into your contact manager. That way you can track the dates on which your releases go out and maintain complete records of contacts with editors and news directors. You can distribute your releases by mail, or use faxes or e-mail to convey immediacy. Journalists at technology publications are generally the most receptive to electronic information, while many others still prefer to receive releases by traditional mail.

Distribute Your Releases Electronically. If you have a broad-based announcement that will be of interest to media in a variety of categories, including general news, you can have your release distributed electronically for a fee via news wire services such as PR Newswire (800-832-5522) and Business Wire (800-221-2462). These services will send your release to thousands of news outlets based on predetermined criteria, such as by type of media. This is an excellent way to ensure the highest distribution for your release, although there is no guarantee the information will be picked up by news media or lead to article placements. And this type of distribution cannot take the place of building one-on-one relationships with select professionals at the media outlets that reach your primary target audience.

▪ Step 3: Develop PR Materials

Now that you know which media you plan to target and the kind of information that will be of greatest interest to their print or broadcast audiences, the third step is to develop your own materials. The most important part of the package is either a press release or a "pitch letter," depending on whether you're sending news or pitching yourself as an expert on a particular topic.

Press Releases and Pitch Letters. To be newsworthy, your press release should contain beneficial information or new information on a timely or relevant issue, identify a trend, or announce an upcoming event. Start off with a headline that states a benefit. This instantly communicates to the journalists, news directors, or assignment editors who receive your release that it's relevant to the needs of their readers, viewers, or listeners. Quantifiable headlines lend credibility to your message. For example, "New Online Ordering System Reduces Office Supply Costs by 20 Percent," or "Online Sales Climb 30 Percent Due to Safety Guarantees," are better headlines than "Smith Office Supply Introduces New Online Ordering System." If you're sending a pitch letter to the media, modify your hook—the lead you use to grab attention—just as you would a press release headline. To continue with the above example, a pitch letter hook might read, "Did you know that new safety measures have increased small business sales online by 30 percent?" Following the hook, explain what your story is about, and why you're qualified to tell it.

Make sure your press release doesn't read like an ad. Stick to the facts and tone down the sales language. It's best to focus on clear communications, using testimonials, expert quotes, and statistics to give weight to your claims. Visually, a straightforward presentation with a simple layout works best. Avoid artful typefaces and graphics that can make your release look like a flyer, and keep it clean and easy to read.

Press Kits. Depending upon the size of your press list, your relationship with the media, and the type of service or product you offer, you may include your press kit along with your release or choose to withhold it and send it only to journalists who respond or contact you for more information. The latter can save you considerable money if your list is quite large. Just be sure to have the kit ready to send out quickly when it's called for.

Years ago, Mark McInturff found the best way to get his foot in the door with a new magazine was to submit photos along with a one-page product description with a built in hook, such as to offer a tour of an award-winning ranch renovation. One advantage his firm has over others who pitch the media is that his staff includes a professional-level photographer, and McInturff believes their work "shows" better because of the quality of the photography they submit with their releases. When McInturff Architects first began its public relations program, the firm would follow the magazines' editorial calendars and send its kits with tie-ins to upcoming features in select issues. Initially, the kits would be put into a pile with two hundred or so others.

But over time, the quality of the firm's press kits helped them to stand out.

Customize your own press kit as appropriate for your business and industry and to meet the needs of the targeted media. Include these basic materials: your press release or pitch letter, a fact sheet, and background information on the story and your company. If the kit accompanies a pitch letter, add information on the types of topics you can address, and your credentials. Include clips from other media, particularly if you're an expert in a given field or to demonstrate your company's abilities in its arena. If you recall, a print article featuring McInturff's work led to television appearances, and additional coverage has led to mentions in books like this one and another on beautiful bedrooms, for example.

▪ Step 4: Build Relationships

The final step in a conventional public relations program is to follow up your releases by telephone and to make regular contact with key media over time. Follow-up is vital. Telephone contact gives you the chance to expand on how your story will benefit the publication's readers or broadcast outlet's listeners or viewers. Be sensitive to the media's deadline pressures and always ask if you've called at a good time. Your goal must be to build relationships and to be on the list of sources that are called upon when there's a need for your particular type of story. After twelve years of pubic relations efforts, McInturff Architects now gets at least one call per year from key magazines to be included in a special feature. True, public relations is "free" publicity until you begin to factor in the cost of the time it takes to win the coverage. But for most businesses, it's clearly worth the effort.

News stories are considered more credible by audiences than advertising, so a single positive story carries a lot of weight. To get more mileage from your coverage, you can purchase reprints of articles for use in your company's marketing program. Your current customers or clients will be impressed and pleased to see your positive coverage, and prospects will be encouraged to work with a firm that's considered expert or a source of valuable news and information.

STAND OUT FROM THE CROWD

While media relations are a vital component of a successful public relations campaign, there are other avenues you can pursue that will gain highly visible publicity for your home-based business.

▪ Publicity from Special Events

Special events are a terrific way to present your work in an environment uncluttered with competing messages—provided you choose the right events or orchestrate your own. For example, Houston-based interior designer Barbara Schlattman contributes her expertise to decorating rooms in show houses to showcase her own abilities and gain publicity and new clients for her firm. The food and beverage industries use special events to introduce new food products, such as prosciutto from Parma or a new type of liquor, to the food and wine press, noted chefs, and cookbook authors.

If you've got a product that is best experienced firsthand, think of ways you can organize a special event to showcase it. Gain the participation of businesses with complementary products. Invite key press to the event, taking care to do pre- and postevent publicity. Hire a professional photographer to take action shots and include a photo with a caption in your postevent publicity. If your event has been used to introduce a new product, shoot color product shots for distribution in slide form in your press kits.

▪ Speaking Engagements

What if you don't market a product that looks great or tastes delicious? Suppose you have a service to promote? Speaking engagements are an ideal way to gain publicity for your company and position yourself as an expert in your field. From *Oprah* to the evening news, media outlets are continually seeking the "expert of the moment" on every conceivable topic and in any field imaginable. Robin Gorman Newman of Great Neck, New York, calls herself a "love coach." Her business is Mensch Finders, and she's the author of *How to Meet a Mensch in New York*. Newman has relied extensively on publicity and speaking engagements to spread the word about her consultations and promote sales of her book. At the time it was published, she was new to public speaking and admits she found it a bit frightening. But now she says nothing has compared to the effectiveness of her speaking engagements, which have led to considerable business for her firm.

Newman believes it's making that personal connection at a speaking engagement that gives you a marketing edge. She relies extensively on press coverage before and after each event. If she is speaking in her home town of Great Neck, for example, Newman contacts the local paper to get a calendar listing to help build attendance at the event. Then she pitches a writer at the paper on covering her talk and writing about her and the book. The event itself becomes the hook for the article. Even in instances where the event itself isn't covered by the media, postevent publicity gives the paper the information it needs to do a follow-up story.

On the opposite coast, in Encinitas, California, Peter Sierck uses speaking engagements to promote an entirely different type of service. His home business, Environmental Testing and Technology, has been in operation thirteen years and has four full-time employees. Sierck's company investigates sick buildings and makes recommendations on what can be done to improve their indoor environments. They perform indoor air quality surveys and test for moisture, mold, electromagnetic fields, radon, asbestos, and other contaminants. Environmental Testing and Technology began by doing residential work (including Madonna's home) and its business now includes commercial work as well. Sierck is often called upon to be an expert witness in court cases and is considered one of the country's leading authorities in his field.

Sierck's structured use of speaking engagements has helped create his standing in the industry and contributed significantly to the growth of his home-based business. He describes this form of public relations as a means of bringing his company's name to the forefront and positioning it as one of the major players in the field. He targets two types of speaking opportunities: associations and groups that are a part of the water restoration industry; and medical conferences for nurses and alternative healthcare providers. Sierck's firm contacts the associations and offers him as a speaker, and he tailors his talks to the needs of each organization.

In turn, his firm receives a list of the participants in each symposium. After Sierck's appearances, Environmental Testing and Technology sends follow-up letters to attendees offering consultation or assistance with environmental services. So Sierck's appearances not only gain publicity through mentions in the programs and any follow-up articles in trade journals, but also offer him a platform to address his most important prospects.

▪ Maximize Your Visibility

As a business owner, you have many chances to participate in community and other events and may be wondering how to choose the best ones for you. Look for opportunities to stand out from the crowd. Instead of participating in six community events in a small way—by sponsoring a runner in a race or taking a small booth in a crowded community fair—choose just one or two events and participate in a way that draws strong attention to your business. The key is to pick only those events that will allow your company's name to stand out and be recognized by a crowd that consists, to a large extent, of your customers and prospects. This works well if you offer a customer service or product. Instead of sponsoring one runner in a series of races, pick the race that will achieve the highest attendance and the most media coverage, and purchase the right to emblazon your company name on the banner at the finish line. In other words, don't merely be a runner—own the race.

CHECKLIST

✓ Decide which target audiences you want to reach through public relations, and determine the kind of information you can offer that they'll find new or noteworthy.

✓ Target the best media to carry your unique message. Plan your public relations list the same way you would an advertising schedule, by researching the media that are looked to as sources of information by your target audience. Public relations give you a chance to place stories where you could not necessarily afford to advertise with enough frequency to penetrate.

✓ Add your public relations list to your contact management software in order to track and maintain an effective program.

✓ Develop your own press releases or pitch letters and an accompanying press kit. Your press release should feature a benefit-oriented headline that makes it immediately apparent to the media that what you have to say will interest their readers, viewers, or listeners. Use the body of the release to explain your message using quotes, statistics, and a straight presentation of the facts, with little hyperbole and sales language. Tailor your press kits to meet the needs of each individual media outlet.

✓ Follow up your releases by telephone and establish a program of ongoing contact with your primary media targets.

✓ Look for opportunities to showcase your company and what it offers in an environment that's relatively uncluttered with competing messages. Consider using speaking engagements to publicize your business and establish you as an expert in your field. (Look for tips on effective speaking in chapter 24.) Use pre- and postevent publicity to get mileage out of each engagement.

✓ Choose special events carefully. Select only those that reach a large percentage of your customers and prospects and give your company maximum visibility.

EIGHTEEN

Create a Terrific Web Site

Truth: Getting off the dirt road and onto the information superhighway can bring a world of new customers to your door.

■ ■ ■

In 1998, Americans with home offices spent $11 billion on Internet access alone. Of that, $5 billion was spent by home-based business owners. To make sense of these numbers, you need to know that in 1998 home offices accounted for a full 68 percent of all U.S. households on the Internet. These and some of the most important statistics on the home office market have been diligently gathered by the prominent research firm International Data Corporation (IDC).

PUT E-MAIL TO WORK

In its report, "Home Offices on the Internet," IDC states that e-mail today is what fax communication was ten years ago. It's not surprising. E-mail communication allows you to increase the visibility for your home-based business, work smoothly with customers no matter where they're based, and reduce the amount of time you spend working with vendors or team members by streamlining communications. It also enables you to sell products worldwide without ever leaving home.

In the overall business landscape, home offices have low visibility. Your prospects are aware of you only when you use marketing tools that reach out to them or sales activities that take you outside your home office. But thanks to the Internet, you can now communicate with prospects and customers or clients across the country and around the world. And you can take the first steps toward increasing your company's visibility with little more than an e-mail account.

▪ Use E-mail As a PR Tool

E-mail is essential if your company must communicate with major corporate clients or customers, and it's an indispensable tool for sharing your work with team members. You can also use e-mail to spread the word about your company by participating in online discussion lists—a form of public relations that can produce extremely positive results. One home business owner, who specializes in facts and information on breast feeding, participates in dozens of discussion lists, and always uses a signature line that includes her name and describes her field of expertise. She contributes content and expert opinions to Web sites that feature information on breast feeding and general topics of interest to new mothers and the medical community. As a result, she is often quoted in online and traditional media and asked to write articles and make appearances to speak on the topic.

▪ E-mail's a Time-Saver

E-mail communication can save you time too. Try capturing the e-mail address for each of your vendors to reduce the amount of time you spend on the telephone. By using e-mail for basic communication, you'll save the time you would normally spend on chitchat. You can also handle your e-mail correspondence with vendors at any time of the day or night no matter where they're located, which would be impossible if you were communicating with them by telephone.

▪ Research Is Easy on the Web

The availability of information on the Internet has transformed the way most companies do research. Although it's important to confirm that the sources of information you find on the Internet are sound, the thousands of research papers, encyclopedias, and directories on the Web have reduced the turnaround on most secondary research projects from weeks to days or hours. In many ways, the Internet is truly leveling the playing field for home-based businesses. Now you have access to much of the same information that was once available only to large firms with major research budgets and staffs with expertise in ferreting out hard-to-find data.

DESIGN AN EFFECTIVE WEB SITE

E-mail communications and research functions just scratch the surface of what can be accomplished on the Web. Web marketing and electronic commerce offer home businesses the chance to reach a world of new customers. A Web site is more than an online brochure. It's a way of setting up an interactive relationship with thousands—or even hundreds of thousands—of prospects. Just a few short years ago, setting up your Web site required a strong knowledge of programming and there was little affordable help available. But now there are low-cost software programs, such as Microsoft FrontPage 2000 and Adobe PageMill 3.0. FrontPage, for example, is a WYSIWYG (what you see is what you get) program that has onscreen wizards to walk you through setting up your Web site in just a matter of hours. It provides professionally designed themes, or graphical templates, that can help you make a polished presentation and avoid design mistakes.

There are also Internet sites that offer free or low-cost Web building tools for "Webmasters," people who set up and maintain Web sites. A comprehensive directory of such sites can be found at http://reallybig.com, which (as I write this) calls itself the "largest directory of Web building resources on the Internet." A recent visit produced links to a huge list of sites that provide everything from graphics and art to buttons that flash and sites that pay referral fees.

One affordable solution is available from Yahoo! Store (http://store.yahoo.com), an e-commerce Web site that gives you access to online tools to customize a prefab store that will join the site's online mall. To simplify matters even further, in 1999 some Internet service providers such as EarthLink (www.earthlink.com) began to offer subscribers Web page hosting and development thanks to built-in software. They also began to facilitate e-commerce at reasonable prices, so home businesses could set up online stores with their own merchant accounts to process secure credit card transactions. It's important to note that not all ISPs can host your Web site. Their primary business is providing Internet access. Web hosting companies specialize in renting space on their servers, and charge fees based on the level of service you require. Some also offer assistance in Web site design.

With so many new sites being added to the Web every day, your site has to provide information, capture the attention of visitors, and make them want to come back time and again for new information. No matter whether you develop your Web site on your own, hire a Web development company, or use a software program, here are some tips for creating a professional-looking site that will enhance your company's image, position you in the minds of visitors, and increase sales for your home-based business.

▪ Make Readability a Top Priority

Short blocks of text work best on the Web. If you have a lot of information to communicate or long articles on your site, introduce them in shorter blocks, then provide visitors the opportunity to get more in-depth information by clicking deeper into your site. Avoid patterned backgrounds and stick with dark type over solid white to ensure readability. The type fonts that show up on the screen may be dependent upon what's included in a viewer's operating system, and the fonts will also be affected by the browser they're viewed on. So stay with standard fonts, and check your site from a variety of browsers. Also, keep your line lengths short to avoid awkward line breaks.

▪ Simplify Navigation

Design a consistent navigation system. This will be easier if you begin by sketching out a schematic of the way information will flow from one page to another on your site. Follow the four click rule—it should take no more than about four mouse clicks for visitors who begin at your main page to find any information they're looking for. Visitors should also be able to tell by looking at your main page what products you sell and how they can get easy access to pricing, product information, and order forms.

▪ Reduce Load Time

Too many bells and whistles—literally too many flashing buttons and large color photographs—can make your site too slow and cumbersome to load quickly. Pages should take no longer than fifteen to thirty seconds to load. If your site must carry a large number of full-color photographs, run them thumbnail-size and let visitors click on the ones they want to enlarge. When pages take too long to load, visitors become impatient and move on.

▪ Make Each Page Self-Sufficient

The software used by most Internet service providers (ISPs) allows visitors to bookmark pages they find of special interest.

That means page four of your site may be the one many visitors choose to bookmark to review later and revisit over time. Each page on your site must be able to stand on its own, with a navigation bar, your company contact information, identification, and copyright. Design your site to make each page self-sufficient so visitors can reach all of your information and products no matter which page they choose to bookmark.

- ### Give Visitors a Reason to Come Back

The Web is a passive medium. Content is king! Visitors must choose to visit your Web site among tens of thousands of others. Continually add to, update, and refresh your site's content to give visitors a reason to return. You don't have to write all of it yourself. You can invite experts to contribute articles, and even hire an editor to coordinate and contribute content for you. Include a simple registration mechanism on your main page that invites visitors to log in their e-mail addresses, and use contests, newsletters (more on this in the coming chapter), and other incentives to persuade them to register. You can include a longer registration form deeper into your site. But you should be aware that the longer your registration form, the less likely visitors will be to complete it.

Philip Hagen, of Hagen Software, Inc., in Fairfax, Virginia, put up his first Web site, www.dcregistry.com, in 1995 while he still had a full-time job as a government attorney. His site was a local community guide that drew traffic (about 350,000 hits a month), though it didn't make much money. While running the site, Hagen made an interesting discovery. He was looking for a way to allow visitors to post classified ads and respond to them on his Web site, but found there were no classified advertising programs available that fit his needs. So back in 1996, he decided to develop his own.

By the summer of 1997, Hagen started selling a program that allowed people to host their own classified sections on their Web sites. The new ready-to-use software enabled the sites built by small- to medium-size companies to compete with those of larger organizations. Encouraged by sales of what was a relatively unpublicized product, Hagen decided to set up a Web site, www.e-classifieds.net, to sell his software programs and he officially gave the products the same name. That was in October of 1998. He got a merchant account and during that same month, sales more than quadrupled. In Hagen's case, by keeping his eyes open he found the need for a product that would help Web businesses like his increase their sales. And he learned a lot from his initial efforts on the DC Registry site.

According to Hagen, with so much competition on the Web, a successful site must be interactive—with mechanisms in place so people can post questions, talk with one another, purchase products, and perhaps even try them out. He has also branded his product with a logo that shows up when someone uses his product on their Web site. For example, when a television station purchases e-Classifieds for use on its site, visitors will see the e-Classifieds logo show up as a live link. So businesspeople who visit Web sites that use Hagen's software can get instant access to information on how they can purchase it for themselves. Within less than one year of launching the e-Classifieds site and selling his products under that name, revenues for Hagen's business are approaching $1 million, and he has now left his position as a government attorney to concentrate on expanding his company.

Hagen's branding technique points out the need for aggressive Web marketing tactics. You'll find more ideas and examples in the next chapter.

CHECKLIST

✓ Starting today, use your e-mail for more than communicating with friends and family. Use it to streamline communications with vendors; send information and work to clients, customers, or team members; and participate in discussion lists.

✓ Get in the habit of using the Web as a research tool. Bookmark sites with content relevant to your type of business, as well as competitors' sites (for ongoing monitoring) and directories or portals that have links to a wide range of sites with news and information.

✓ If you don't already have a Web site for your business, consider the ways you could use it as a marketing tool to sell products or as an income generator for your firm. Follow the guidelines in this chapter to create a user-friendly site that's easy to read, loads quickly, and gives visitors a reason to come back. Use affordable software, a Web design company, or help from an ISP to create a professional-looking site that meets your company's goals.

NINETEEN

Market Your Web Site

Truth: The secret to a successful Web site is to keep visitors coming back for more.

■ ■ ■

Success on the Web relies on two critical elements: drawing visitors to your site and persuading them to return. Since the Web is a passive medium (visitors must type in your address to visit your site) it's up to you to generate traffic. And the best sites in the world won't succeed if no one knows about them. An effective campaign is absolutely essential when selling products on the Web or maintaining an advertiser-supported site.

Your Web hosting company can generally provide you with statistics on the number of hits per day your site receives and how many pages are viewed daily, weekly, or monthly. But it's equally important what visitors *do* when they get there. If you're carrying advertising on your site, your ad rates may be based on the number of visitors in a given period, or the amount of click-throughs an advertiser gets on its banner or icon. Your site can also earn referral commissions by displaying logos with live links to other sites that pay fees for the customers you produce for them.

▪ It's All In the Domain Name

To generate sufficient traffic for your site, start by choosing a recognizable domain name. The right name can make it easier for visitors to find you. So select one that's as close to the name of your company or product as possible. You can check the availability of any domain name you choose by doing a quick search thanks to Network Solutions at www.networksolutions.com. Register your domain name either through your ISP or directly with Network Solutions for just seventy dollars for two years. Even if you're not quite ready to set up your own Web site, it's always a good idea to register the name you want, just so it doesn't get nabbed by a competitor.

THE BEST WAYS TO PROMOTE YOUR SITE

▪ Register with Search Engines

Make your site easy to find. Suppose you were selling Native American jewelry, for example. Many prospects would find your site by searching on engines such as Yahoo!, Excite, and Lycos. You can register with the major search engines by visiting each one's site and filling out its forms, but this can be a time-consuming process. So you may want to use a company such as LinkExchange, Inc., to do it for you instead. By visiting its site (www.linkexchange.com) and clicking on "Submit It!," you can purchase a twelve-month license with unlimited access and re-submissions for two Web addresses (called URLs). Submit It! offers a master form on which you enter your keywords, description, and complete information about your Web site for submission to forty search engines.

While registering with search engines is important, don't count on them to be your primary traffic generator. The most well-established sites, and those which have the greatest number of hits, are the ones to receive the highest rankings when searches are performed. If your site is new and you're trying to attract your first visitors, chances are good it will be number fifty or sixty to show up in a search. By the time searchers have been through the first page of links, they'll have what they're searching for or will have given up, and your lower-ranking site will rarely be noticed.

▪ Promote Your URL in Company Materials

To make your site easy for your own customers and qualified prospects to locate, promote it in all your company materials. Prominently display your URL on your business cards, letterhead, brochures, flyers, and ads. If you have a newsletter, add the URL to the masthead and put in a special feature about your site. Look for ways you can use other media to promote your online efforts, such as by mailing a special postcard to your customers or clients.

▪ Set Up Links, Banner Ads, and Affiliate Programs

Promote your site online by setting up links to and from related sites. Not sure which sites attract your target audience? To get a comprehensive list, do a keyword search and see what turns up or use the SRDS directory *Interactive Advertising Source*. Like all the SRDS reference tools, you'll find it at major libraries and available by subscription at www.srds.com. Look at related (though not directly competitive) sites and contact their Webmasters to set up reciprocal links. Be sure to negotiate for descriptive text to accompany your link. Your targeted sites may contain long lists of "hot links" and visitors will read the descriptive text to decide which to visit next.

Web advertising—even on quality sites—can be surprisingly inexpensive. You can purchase banner ads on high-traffic sites that reach your target audience, or set up an affiliate program to run your hot-linked logo on a variety of home pages that can help drive traffic to your site. There are also sites, such as www.doubleclick.net, that allow you to place advertising with online networks. For a comprehensive look at ad networks and representation firms, use the *Interactive Advertising Source* directory.

The Microsoft site LinkExchange, mentioned above, is one of the best places to start for a full range of services to market your Web site. It offers advertising space on more than four hundred thousand Web sites, ClickTrade for creating affiliate programs, and a banner network, among other accessible services. Another top-flight resource is online at www.internet.com. The internet.com Network is organized into nine areas of content, including an Internet marketing channel. Click on "Ad Resource" for a library of advertising and marketing links, or "Refer-It" for a directory of affiliate and referral programs as well as information on banner exchanges. In addition to setting up an affiliate program to place your hot-linked logo on other sites, you may also want to set aside space on your own site to carry affiliate advertising. As you build traffic, the income from your affiliate advertising can help offset the cost of your site.

Melisse Shapiro and her agent couldn't get a publisher to buy her novel, *Lip Service*, until her grass-roots marketing campaign on the Web drew major attention to the book. Within four months, she went from being a frustrated writer to being an excited author when Doubleday Direct purchased book club rights for *Lip Service*. Shortly thereafter, sale of the remaining rights went to Pocket Books.

Shapiro mounted her online marketing assault from her home office in Greenwich, Connecticut, where she spent most every day at her computer (with a dog curled in her lap) working the Web. She began by setting up a Web site, www.ReadLipService. com, which carried chapter one of her novel, then self-published. Readers could purchase the complete book via electronic file or order a print on demand copy for nine dollars. Shapiro concentrated her marketing efforts on finding Web sites that drew women, her primary target audience. Beginning with the owners of smaller, less-well-known sites, she offered free copies of the book for review or for use as contest prizes, and articles for their sites in exchange for publicity. Each review posted on one site was sent in an e-mail letter to other, larger sites. Shapiro also opened discussion lists to talk about her novel and similar works in the same genre. Everything she posted included her signature line with her pseudonym, "MJ Rose, author of *Lip Service*," and a live link to her Web site.

Shapiro's campaign, which was begun in November, won her publicity on sixty sites by February. About that time, the novel was discovered online by a Doubleday editor and chosen as a featured alternate for the Book Club and Literary Guild. When that happened, Shapiro fired off a release by e-mail to the wire services, which resulted in interviews in *Newsweek* and *Entertainment Weekly*. Jumping on the opportunity to capitalize on the press coverage, Shapiro's agent sent copies of the manuscript to publishers who, this time, were willing to bid. And in March, Pocket Books became Shapiro's publisher.

▪ Use Traditional Media

Publicity in print and other media can be a traffic generator too. Many publications, even those that don't regularly cater to a Web-based audience, now carry at least a column of critique and commentary on new and interesting Web sites. If your new site is truly unique, unusually comprehensive, or in some way noteworthy, use public relations strategies to gain media placements that will drive traffic to your site. When communicating with journalists who write about the Web, you can use more eye-catching and innovative tactics than for other media. Try sending your release electronically with a live link to your Web site. Then follow up by telephone.

With a solid program in place to bring visitors to your site, you can take advantage of proven techniques that keep them coming back for more. Without a mechanism to remind your target audience that your site exists, you simply have to sit back and hope they remember to make return visits. One of the most powerful tools for building return visits is an electronic news-letter.

BUILD INTERACTION WITH AN ELECTRONIC NEWSLETTER

A terrific electronic newsletter supplies information that's of special interest to subscribers and stimulates returns to your site. The most important goal is to create interactivity, and your electronic newsletter provides a powerful vehicle for building relationships with your prospects. The first step is to build a registration form into your site as recommended in the last chapter. Then send your newsletter to your subscriber base. Newsletters should be sent only to those who've requested them. It's also a good idea to record the date on which each person subscribes to avoid any unfounded accusations of "spamming" (sending electronic junk mail). And make sure your newsletter goes out with enough frequency, or readers may forget they've subscribed.

The Mailing List. At the outset when your list is small—say, several hundred subscribers—you can send out the newsletter yourself using just about any Internet service provider. You'll have to break your list into groups of fifty, so that it won't be rejected by your ISP as spam. To send the newsletter, address it to yourself and put your list in the "bcc" field. Of course, with a larger list of several thousand names or more, it's best to use a list hosting company. One of the principal advantages of working with a hosting firm is that it will deal with undeliverable mail and keep the list clean and updated. You can expect your costs to begin at several hundred dollars a month, depending upon the level of service you need.

A Few More Tips. It's not essential to create all of the content for your electronic newsletter yourself. You can enlist the services of experts or hire an editor. Graphically, the newsletter should be readable for all subscribers. So it's best to place hard returns after every sixty characters or less and keep your newsletter in plain text with no boldface or underlines.

Consider Making It a Profit Center. Once your newsletter reaches a large enough subscriber base, it may become an attractive advertising vehicle. In fact, as your electronic newsletter grows more successful, it can become a stand-alone profit center for your company, just as it did for Lauren MacDonald. She's the cofounder of the Monthly Buzz, an e-mail newsletter and Web site specifically designed to provide young professionals with information on their local social scene.

MacDonald and a partner started the Monthly Buzz in September 1995 as a print publication in Washington, D.C., and later created the Web site and e-mail newsletter in October 1996. They now have twenty-five thousand subscribers in Washington, D.C., a separate list for the Delaware beaches with twenty thousand subscribers, and have just begun a Baltimore newsletter. The Monthly Buzz newsletter is published twice a month and contains more in-depth information than the Web site, though both cover fun things to do and special events with an emphasis on the club and bar scene.

The Monthly Buzz also features local, on-premise promotions in conjunction with sponsors. They shoot fun digital photographs at each of the promotional events and post them on the Web site so participants can visit to see themselves partying with their friends and newcomers can be enticed to get in on the fun. This builds interactivity between the site, the newsletter, and their subscribers. MacDonald keeps people coming back because she maintains a good balance between content and advertising. Like MacDonald's, your own electronic newsletter must have strong, worthwhile content. With so many newsletters vying for your target audience's attention, your subscribers will keep reading yours only so long as it meets their unique needs.

MacDonald designed the site herself, but now uses Microsoft FrontPage to update it. She and her two employees write all the content. MacDonald views the electronic newsletter as basically a direct mail piece that calls on twenty-five thousand people at their desks—she's not sitting back waiting for twenty-five thousand people to visit her Web site. And advertisers such as Miller Brewing Company, Club Med, and Bacardi as well as local businesses support the newsletter because it delivers their target audience and keeps them coming back.

CHECKLIST

✓ Draw visitors to your site by choosing an easily recognizable domain name and by making your site easy to find. Register with search engines, but don't expect them to be your primary traffic generator.

✓ Promote your site in all of your company materials and by setting up links to and from related sites. Display your URL on all of your business cards, brochures, ads, and flyers and use special promotions to make your customers and prospects aware of your new site. Set up reciprocal links between your site and others that reach the same target audience.

✓ Negotiate for and place advertising on high-traffic sites that reach your prospects. Use traditional media, too, to gain publicity, by submitting an electronic press release to media that carry critique and commentary on new and interesting Web sites.

✓ Use an electronic newsletter as a powerful vehicle to keep visitors coming back or as a separate profit center for your company. Send your newsletter only to those who subscribe, either on your own—if your list is small—or with the help of a list hosting company.

✓ Create interactivity between your Web site and the newsletter. And be certain to provide content that's of continuing interest to your target audience, striking a good balance between content and advertising messages.

TWENTY

Win More Referrals

Truth: The key to winning referrals is knowing whom, and how, to ask.

. . .

Ann Cochran's business, Applied Communications, was founded and built on referrals. The six-year-old corporate communications firm got its start when Cochran set out to look for a new job. A friend referred her to the National Institutes of Health, but the department there was in a hiring freeze, so her prospective employer asked her to create a newsletter on a freelance basis. When the hiring freeze continued for months, Cochran asked her "client" if there were other departments within NIH who might need her services. He made a referral that won Cochran another client, and her business was born.

It's a common misconception that if your business does terrific work, referrals will come in automatically. It's true, word of mouth is a good way to build a business, but you'll have much greater results if you know the right people to ask and how to approach them for the referrals you need. A recent study by the Nierenberg Group, in New York City, showed that sales and marketing professionals often consider referrals the most effective technique for attracting new customers. The survey included nine hundred professionals who rated sales and marketing techniques on a scale of one to five, with five being "very important" and one being "not important." Referrals got an average rating of 4.8, followed closely by one-to-one sales with a rating of 4.5. The study revealed that sales and marketing professionals find the quickest way to build business is to ask existing customers or clients for referrals to others who will have a need for what they offer.

BUILD A REFERRAL PROGRAM

Current customers or clients and businesses that serve your target audience are your two best sources of referrals. But they can't make referrals if they aren't aware when people need you, don't know how or when to refer business to you, or don't remember you. So it's important to remind customers and others that you're interested in referrals, and put programs in place to keep your business fresh in their minds. Make a habit of letting clients know what you need. Be direct and say something such as, "Much of my business is built on referrals. Do you know of anyone who would like to receive high-quality service?" Or try asking, "I have room in my schedule for a little more work; do you know someone who might need . . . ?"

- **Stay in Touch**

Make a habit of asking for referrals in writing as well. If you regularly distribute a survey or follow-up form at the completion of a project, include a request for referrals. For many businesses that rely on repeat sales from the same customer or client base, staying "top-of-mind" is of principal importance. Have an ongoing marketing strategy in place to regularly communicate with past clients or customers—just as you do with your prospect database. Not only will this group be a source of repeat business, but by reminding past customers or clients of the good work you did together and your ongoing ability to meet their needs, you'll prompt them to refer business your way as well. Send your customer list an electronic or broadcast fax newsletter with an overview of current projects and helpful information, or send regular postcard mailings to keep in touch. And periodically call past clients to maintain ongoing relationships.

■ Target Referral Sources

Throughout this book, you've seen examples of ways to set up marketing programs to reach people in businesses that serve your target audience. These referral sources should be considered a primary or secondary target audience for your home-based business. Remember the mortgage broker in chapter 11 who called on Realtors in order to build referrals to prospective homeowners? And in chapter 25 we'll discuss a writer who formed a marketing partnership with a designer in order to collaborate and share referrals.

Referral relationships are built one by one over time. Would you refer business to someone you didn't know much about? Use telephone calls and, in some industries, e-mail to establish the first contact with a businessperson you believe will become a good referral source. Then ask to drop by their office and talk about referrals, or offer to meet for lunch or coffee where you can get to know each other and share stories or work samples. It should always be clear that you're meeting for the purpose of talking about gaining referrals, and you should be prepared to offer referrals in return.

■ Network Selectively

Ann Cochran joined her local chamber of commerce and several other organizations but found that general networking wasn't producing the quantity of referrals she was looking for. So she joined a formal organization that puts together networking groups of twenty-five to thirty people. Each member pays several hundred dollars a year to join and attend weekly meetings. Cochran describes her group as very leads-driven. Members are encouraged to invite guests and at each meeting stand and give a thirty-second introduction or overview of their businesses. During the meeting, each person must give at least one lead to another member of the group. On weeks when Cochran doesn't have a lead to share, she's asked to give a testimonial about someone in the group whose services she's used. For Cochran, each meeting produces at least one lead for her corporate communications business and she finds it an excellent addition to the two major ongoing clients she serves.

Networking, whether through leads clubs or other organizations, is a great way to initiate contact with cold prospects. You don't have to wait until you're in a formal business setting to network. In fact, you can make great contacts at the ballpark or waiting in line at the movies. But for most home-based business owners, business and professional groups provide the main source of contacts. Choose your groups carefully. You may want to attend several meetings of each group under consideration prior to anteing up your dues. Look for groups that enable you to network one-on-one with your prospects or with business owners who can refer clients or customers.

Be an Active Participant. It's not enough to join several organizations and sit quietly through occasional meetings. To get any benefit out of your memberships, you have to be willing to participate actively in meetings or functions. Reach out to people you don't know. Move around the room, introducing yourself. When someone asks, "What do you do?" don't simply tell them you're a CPA, a home remodeler, or a jewelry designer, for example, or you'll lose the chance to help them learn more about your business. Your answer to that simple question should stimulate conversation and provide a memorable hook. It's best to prepare in advance a clear introduction of yourself that helps people understand what you do. What do you want people to know about you? Suppose you're a Realtor who is looking for listings and someone asks what you do. You might say, "I help people sell their homes fast at a great price." Or if your goal is to generate buyers for your listings, you might say, "I help families find the right homes in great neighborhoods."

When networking in a group setting like this, encourage others to talk about what they do. Ask questions and listen (with focused intent) to what they tell you. Referral relationships are based on mutual trust. You'll lay a solid foundation when each person you encounter feels you care about their needs and the ways you can work together.

Just as you developed an intriguing introduction, go to each networking meeting with a clear agenda—a focused idea of what you want people to remember about you and do as a result. You'll have limited time to speak with a number of individuals in a typical networking setting. By planning in advance the key points you want to communicate, you'll find it easier to work them into your conversations. Suppose you're a registered nurse and midwife attending a meeting of a professional women's group. Instead of enumerating the wide range of services your practice provides, you might decide to focus on building attendance at your classes for parents-to-be when the women you meet ask about your business.

Follow Up. After networking sessions, follow up by telephone or mail with the key contacts you wish to pursue. Then add them to your database for future contact.

▪ Don't Overlook Your Competitors

Colleagues (yes, that's right, your competitors) can also be a good source of referrals for your home-based business. It helps if you have a specialty or niche and can make your colleagues aware of your efforts to bring in customers or clients looking for expertise in your area of specialization. Establish relationships with your colleagues built on mutual trust and referrals. You can send the work you're too busy to take on to someone you know will do a good job, and each of you will benefit from referrals in your own specialties.

▪ Some More Important Tips on Referrals

• When looking for referrals, be specific about what you want. You have to train people to think about you.

• It's generally best to let someone know when you're giving their name as a referral prospect. This will help preserve the positive relationship you have with the individual—whether they are a customer or client or a friend—and will also pave the way for the individual to whom you've made the referral.

• Follow up on referrals promptly, then get back to the person who gave you the lead to keep them apprised of your progress. This will give them the confidence to send more referrals your way.

• Ask all new clients or customers where they heard about your business. If the lead has come via a referral, call the person who sent the prospect to you and say thanks, or send a personal note.

Referrals are your "hottest" prospects. They have a need for what you offer and a high regard for you based on their relationship with the person who made the referral. So give them top-flight service and care.

CHECKLIST

✓ Make your current customers or clients aware you're interested in referrals. Use ongoing marketing tools, such as newsletters and postcards, as well as telephone calls to remind them of the quality products and services you offer. Ask for referrals at the completion of major projects or when distributing follow-up surveys or forms.

✓ Identify good referral sources and make them a primary or secondary target audience. Initiate contacts by telephone and set up meetings to talk about referrals with colleagues or business owners that reach your target audience. Be clear about the purpose of your meetings, and be prepared to offer referrals in return.

✓ Explore membership in a lead group in your area. Look for other networking opportunities that bring you into one-on-one contact with your prospects or individuals who can send business your way.

✓ For networking purposes, prepare an introduction of yourself that stimulates conversation. Remember to focus your conversations on the key things you want people to remember about you.

✓ Take great care of referral prospects because they've come to you ready to make a buying decision. Handle referrals well, and it will reflect positively on the contacts who sent them to you and stimulate additional referrals.

TWENTY-ONE

Plot Your Strategies and Tactics

Truth: It takes three types of prospects—cold, warm, and hot—to fuel a healthy business.

■ ■ ■

Does this sound familiar? You're so busy doing your work you have no time for marketing. You work very hard for three months, six months, or even a year, and suddenly look around and realize you may have worked yourself out of a job. You've finished the project that you have in-house or completed all the client or customer orders. So you begin marketing nonstop for three months, or six months, until you bring in some work. Then you say to yourself, "Whew, now I can stop marketing," and you begin the cycle all over again. Work hard for months, market hard for months, work hard, market hard. As a result, you end up living on an economic roller coaster. It's always feast or famine, because you only market in the slow times.

The secret to winning customers year-round is to get off the economic roller coaster and set up a proactive marketing program for your home-based business that you can manage along with day-to-day operations. There are several types of businesses that have at least one period during the year when it's virtually impossible to do any marketing, such as CPAs and accountants who handle tax preparation. But in the majority of situations, continuous, ongoing marketing can be clearly linked to steady growth for most businesses.

Take the case of a fellow I'll call Matthew, a talented graphic designer who, after working eight years in advertising agencies, decided to start his own freelance business. He started out with his old agency as his primary client. He also partnered on projects creating marketing materials for small businesses with a copywriter who had left the agency a year before. Between the two sources, he had enough work to keep himself busy and an income close to what he'd been earning as an agency employee.

Then at the end of his first year as a freelancer, Matthew hit a bump in the road. The agency he had freelanced for lost a major account and stopped sending him assignments, and he didn't have enough work from teaming with his copywriter friend to sustain his income. So he began looking for other clients, something he might have begun a year before. First he contacted old friends, and eventually he used direct mail to reach targeted businesses. His marketing efforts began to bear fruit, but it took a good six months, and by that time he had gone through much of his savings.

Once again, Matthew applied himself to the work at hand, setting marketing aside until, several months later, he found himself in the same boat. That's when Matthew came to understand what every successful business owner knows. To build a steady income from any home-based business, you must have an ongoing, proactive marketing program that you work day in and day out.

Here's another important business truth: To win the business you need, you must be willing to ask for it. You must also ask the right people the right way. You can't sit by the phone like a hopeful teenager waiting for it to ring.

If you're like most home business owners, you started your

business using your own money instead of borrowing from a bank or other lender, or you may have borrowed money from family and friends. Typically, home business owners who start out this way tend to skip over creating business plans, and most importantly they never create an ongoing marketing program.

The majority of home-based business owners have had little or no experience calling on prospects or making sales before starting their companies. And my goal is not to turn you into a salesperson. Instead it's to arm you with the tools you need to create a fulfilling lifestyle for you and your family and ensure your long-term future. According to an *Inc.* magazine survey, the owners of the fastest growing businesses in America with sales of one million dollars or less spend an average of 37 percent of their time in sales and marketing each week. So if you're spending less than about 40 percent of your time asking for the business in one way or another, you're probably not doing all you can to increase your income and support your new lifestyle. And if you're just starting your business, you may need to spend 60 percent of your time or more in sales and marketing.

YOUR SALES CYCLE

Every home-based business owner has three kinds of prospects—cold, warm, and hot. Visualize them for a moment as though they were moving through your sales cycle the way hands on a clock move from twelve o'clock all the way around the dial and back to twelve again. Your coldest prospects are from noon to about two o'clock on the dial. These are businesses or individuals you've added to your prospect list or who may be members of your target audience, but they know little or nothing about your company.

Warm prospects are from about two or three to eight o'clock on the sales cycle dial. These prospects are more familiar with your company. Perhaps they've seen your advertising, spoken with you on the telephone, received your direct mail, or met with you in the past. Your hottest prospects are from about eight o'clock to midnight on the dial. These have come to you either as referrals—they've heard great things about you and are ready to be convinced that you can provide the benefits they're looking for—or you've successfully moved them through your sales cycle from cold to warm then hot.

CREATE AN ONGOING MARKETING PROGRAM

It takes an average of eight contacts with a prospect before a sale is closed. That means it will take multiple contacts with prospects as you move them through the sales cycle from cold to warm and eventually to hot. So in the past, if you've picked up the telephone and contacted prospects and they've said, "Well, I'm not really interested right now," and you've taken them off your list, you missed out on opportunities to grow your home-based business.

To be successful, your marketing program must reach out to prospects in all three stages—cold, warm, and hot—throughout the sales cycle. Don't make the mistake of using only the marketing tactics with which you're most comfortable. For example, one home-based business owner I know enjoys networking and goes to lots of meetings, initiating contact with prospects. But she rarely moves them through the sales cycle because she doesn't use any other sales or marketing tactics. On the other hand, I know a fellow who is extremely uncomfortable going out and meeting with prospects. So he focuses all of his efforts on direct marketing. He'll send out package after package, always reaching out to just the warm group of prospects. He never cultivates new prospects through interpersonal relationships and often fails to move prospects from warm to hot.

The secret to winning new customers or clients year-round is to set up a proactive program that combines interpersonal interaction, the one-on-one stuff, with marketing to wider groups. Take Carol Curtis and Peter Deutsch, for example. They're the owners of Creative Bird Accessories of Darien, Connecticut, which specializes in sales of products for exotic bird financiers. Curtis and Deutsch created a well-rounded, on-going marketing program for their home business that proved so successful they recently finalized a merger with a major pet supply cataloguer. The centerpiece of their program was a high-quality, seventy-two–page color catalog, featuring everything from clothing, jewelry, artwork, and videos to bird toys, perches, and cages. Thanks to a well-maintained database, Curtis and Deutsch mailed 130,000 copies of the catalog to a qualified list. They also operated a Web catalog, participated in between nine and thirteen "bird shows" per year, and advertised in trade publications, including *Bird Talk*, *Pet News*, and *Just Parrots*, which is published in England and Germany.

In all, Curtis and Deutsch would take orders via their toll-free number, by mail, in person at shows, from the Internet, and by fax. And no matter how customers found them, they carefully tracked which of their sales and marketing tactics produced results. Deutsch could even tell you which products sold best using a particular tactic.

▪ Use Multiple Tactics

If you're relying on a single tactic or perhaps just one or two, it's time to mix it up a bit. Since it may take eight contacts with a prospect or more before a sale is closed, you'll need to adopt a variety of cold, warm, and hot sales and marketing tactics. But don't worry, there are enough to choose from. In the next few pages I'll share a handy formula.

When I was growing up, once a week we'd go to our neighborhood Chinese restaurant for a big family dinner. Perhaps you did too. Remember how you used to order two items from column A, two from column B, and two from column C? Setting up an ongoing marketing program is a lot like that. You can choose two sales and marketing tactics that reach cold prospects, two that reach warm, and two more that reach your hottest prospects. That way, you can set up an annual schedule and be confident you're moving prospects through the sales cycle from cold to warm to hot.

Two sales tactics that reach cold prospects are networking and cold calling. Marketing tactics include advertising, PR, Web marketing, and direct mail. So if you're targeting other businesses, you might choose networking and public relations as the two tactics to reach your coldest prospects. Advertising, PR, direct mail, and Web sites are also excellent tools for reaching out to warm prospects. So if you were already using a PR program you could continue it on a variety of levels to reach your warm prospects too. To complete your choice of two warm tactics, you might add direct mail or choose to use electronic newsletters, broadcast faxes, or sales tactics such as meetings and follow-up calls to reach warm prospects.

Hot marketing tactics are those that add a feeling of immediacy, such as faxes and e-mails. Personal, one-on-one interaction adds the final heat to close most sales. That means you'll probably either meet with prospects, perhaps going through the entire proposal and presentation stages, or talk with your prospects on the telephone in order to close them.

Look through the list in the chart on page 182, and choose one sales and one marketing tool or tactic from each category.

▪ Schedule Time Realistically

Which of the tactics in the chart will you select to reach your goals? Before you make a final decision, think about how much time will be required to carry out the tactics you've selected. It's important to create a plan that includes a combination of sales and marketing tactics you can comfortably engage in year-round to support the growth of your home-based business. (You'll find a step-by-step guide to writing a marketing plan in the next chapter.)

PROSPECT TYPE

SALES TACTICS

Cold	Warm	Hot
Cold calling	Follow-up calls	Presentations
Networking	Meetings	Meetings
	Sales letters	Telephone calls
	Sales literature	Proposals
	E-mail	Estimates
	Networking	Contracts

MARKETING TACTICS

Cold	Warm	Hot
Advertising	Advertising	E-mail
Public relations	Public relations	Faxes
Direct mail	Direct mail	
Telemarketing	Broadcast faxes	
Seminars	Electronic newsletter	
Special promotions	Web site	
Trade shows		
Web site		

Suppose your prospective clients are other businesses and your sales strategy includes contacting twenty per week by telephone. You'll also have to schedule time to handle the results, such as the five meetings that will result from the twenty phone calls; the ten packages of follow-up information to be mailed; and the callbacks to the rest of the twenty you were unable to reach the first time. If you plan twenty calls for the first week, you should also expect to be dealing with the follow-up for three weeks or perhaps longer. So, depending on your typical client load, instead of scheduling twenty new business telephone calls per week, you might choose to schedule twenty calls every *other* week.

Here's another example. Let's say you're marketing to consumers, and you decide to use a direct mail campaign to make initial contact with a qualified list of consumer prospects. Since the typical positive response rate in direct mail is 1 to 5 percent, you plan to mail five thousand packages with the assistance of a letter shop. And let's say all goes well. You use a high-quality, well-cleaned list and an effective, professionally produced direct marketing campaign, with a convincing call to action. As a result, your program yields a solid 1 percent response. That's fifty prospect responses. It's essential to schedule the time that will be required to complete the selling cycle using telephone calls, and perhaps meetings, to close a percentage of those respondents.

Now, let's say your typical close rate is 50 percent. If you're selling a consumer product that, once sold, requires little or no additional effort or follow-up, you may be comfortable making twenty-five sales per mailing. On the other hand, if you market a consumer service that your home-based business will provide over time, then gaining twenty-five new customers or clients all at once may be much more than your firm can handle. Instead of mailing five thousand packages at once, you'd be better off mailing a small quantity per week and possibly adding follow-up telephone contact (limited, personalized telemarketing). That one-two punch would be more manageable for your home-based service business, and could actually increase your closure rate.

It's easy to see why, no matter which tactics you choose, it's vital to think through all the steps in advance in order to create a workable program you can manage consistently and comfortably over time. The bottom line is to plan ahead and plot your tactics in your contact management software program (see chapter 9) or on your calendar. Then block out time as if you were scheduling customer or client activity—and stick to it!

CHECKLIST

✓ If you've been in business a while, look back over the past months and ask yourself whether you've been marketing only when you absolutely had no other choice, just when you had a chance, or when there was not much else to do. Make a decision today to change the way you structure your time to include an ongoing marketing program.

✓ Divide your prospect list into three groups—cold, warm, and hot. Begin thinking about which marketing tactics you'll use to move each group closer to a buying decision.

✓ Based on an understanding of your own unique business, choose a sales tactic from each group in the chart that will move prospects closer to a buying decision. Make sure to select the tactics that will have the greatest success, not just those you're comfortable with. For example, if you're marketing to other businesses, but are worried about your cold calling abilities, don't just avoid the tactic. Learn all you can about using the telephone and polish your skills. (More in chapter 11.)

✓ Choose a marketing tool or tactic from each of the categories in this chapter's chart. Plot your sales and marketing activities in a contact management program or on a calendar. Then have a long, hard look. Are you taking on more than you can manage along with the regular operations of your company? It's always better to begin with a modest program, achieve a measure of success, and then build on what works. See the next chapter for a guide to formalizing your marketing plan.

TWENTY-TWO

Write Your Marketing Plan

Truth: Taking shortcuts when it comes to a marketing plan can short-circuit your home-based business.

■ ■ ■

Some friends of ours were building their dream house. They'd waited for years and were finally in a position to build the kind of home they'd always wanted to suit the needs of their growing family. As you can imagine, there were countless meetings with the builder and a long list of choices to make on everything from countertops to floors. Our friends had to decide just how big their structure would be and what it would look like. They made decisions on the types of materials that would be used, and approved their cost. And along the way, their builder used a step-by-step printout of the activity necessary to get the structure completed on time and within budget.

Putting your business on a success track is a lot like building a dream house. Marketing is a cornerstone in the foundation of your home-based business. Without it, nothing happens. And the truth is, you can't build your future without a plan.

CREATE A WORKABLE PLAN

The process of creating a marketing plan is a lot like constructing a new home. There are so many alternatives to choose from. If you've ever gone to your local home center store to do something as simple as select a new bathroom faucet, you understand what I mean. You probably encountered as many choices there—faucets in every style, size, make, and model—as you will when setting up your marketing program. Should you use direct mail? How often should you mail, and to whom? What about advertising—if you use print advertising, should it be classified or display? What about a referral program? And which marketing tools will be best for your business?

Fortunately, here you are reading chapter 22, and by now you know everything you need to create a terrific marketing plan. (Yes, you do!) Each of the preceding twenty-one truths has given you a piece of information you can use to increase your success. If you reviewed the checklists and followed the advice and guidelines you found in each chapter, you're entirely prepared to create your own marketing program.

Here's a list of what you *now* know about marketing your business:

- How to find out what your competitors are doing.

- The best ways to position against them.

- How to focus your efforts on your most qualified prospects.

- How to develop prospect lists, build leads, and win referrals.

- The types of tools you'll need for sales and marketing.

- What your tools must communicate in order to motivate prospects.

- Which strategies you'll adopt for your ongoing sales and marketing program.

- How to select and buy advertising and direct mail lists.

- Which PR tactics make the most sense for you.

- How to use the Internet to market your business.

- The approximate budget you'll set aside for marketing.

Right now, all this information is just rattling around in your head. It won't become useful until it's translated into an action plan, like the step-by-step chart of activity a builder follows to complete a home as specified. If your plan isn't written down, there's little chance you'll stick to it. There's so much competing for your attention every hour of the day. Clients or customers call; there's work to finish and deadlines to meet. Without a written plan, you'll quickly lose your way.

Write a marketing plan to incorporate into your business plan when starting your company. Or if you have an established business, write a stand-alone marketing plan to keep you on track. It should be brief, clear, and to the point. Use an outline or bullet points to convey your information, particularly if this document is for your personal use only. If your written program will be part of a business plan you'll use to qualify for funding, include more details to make it clear to readers who are less familiar with your business exactly what your goals are and how you will achieve them.

▪ Begin with a Situation Analysis

Your annual sales and marketing plan will start with an overview, or *situation analysis*. That's a realistic look at your competition and position in the marketplace. Write a brief description of who your competitors are and how you'll position against them. Be clear about the specific challenges your business will face in the coming year, and describe in just a few short sentences the unique characteristics that set your company apart, your market niche, and the benefits you offer as discussed in chapter 1. This way, when you review this plan in a year's time, you'll easily see how your position has changed and why.

■ Describe Your Target Audience

The second section is a simple, brief description of your target audience. Exactly who is this program designed to reach? If you're marketing to consumers, include a target audience profile with your prospects' demographics here as explained in chapter 8. Business-to-business marketers should describe your targeted business categories and any special qualifying criteria for prospects in each one. Refer back to chapters 3 and 7 for the basics on how.

■ List Your Goals

Section three of your plan is a concise, bulleted list of your sales and marketing *goals* for your business. Make them quantifiable, with a precise deadline for completion, so you can give yourself a well-deserved pat on the back as you achieve them. State specifically what you plan to accomplish, such as, "Increase sales by 10 percent by March 1, 25 percent by June 30, and 50 percent by year-end." It's better to set a goal such as, "Win three medical accounts by September 1," for example, than to simply plan to "develop medical sales," because you'll be able to evaluate your results at a fixed point in time.

■ Outline Your Strategies and Tactics

Your next step is to describe exactly how you'll achieve these goals. Section four contains your marketing *strategies*—the bulk of your sales and marketing plan. This strategies section outlines precisely what activities you plan to undertake and the tools you'll produce in order to make your projected sales and achieve your list of goals. Above all, be realistic. Avoid the temptation to put too much into your program. In fact, the planning process itself is a great way to avoid overcommitment, because once you see your tactics laid out on paper or on your computer screen, you'll know at a glance if you're taking on too much. Your objective is to adopt strategies that will help you generate leads and close sales. But the tactics required must be manageable along with the day-to-day operations of your home-based business.

Throughout this book, you've been exposed to many different strategies and tactics for marketing and by now have a clear understanding of those that will require the greatest "hands-on" commitment. Most sales tactics, including networking, building a referral program, cold calling, and meetings and presentations, are more time intensive than marketing activities, such as postcard mailings, display advertising, and sending press kits. To help ensure your long-term commitment and execution of your plan, select a combination of sales and marketing tactics (refer to chapter 21) that will require varying levels of personal time to supervise and carry out. Then complete the strategies section of your plan by clearly delineating all the steps you'll take to market your company in the coming year.

▪ Finalize a Budget

Next, attach costs to each of your tactics and complete the final section, your marketing *budget*. You'll undoubtedly have to do some homework to get the necessary pricing information. Contact printers for estimates and review media kits for advertising rates, for example. Don't forget to include the small stuff, which can really mount up! Suppose you regularly send out large information kits in plastic folders to well-qualified prospects. It's easy to overlook the cost of the folders and shipping when formulating your budget.

If you find the tactics you've built into your plan require a higher budget than you can realistically support, go back and reevaluate them and look for other, more affordable ways of reaching your goals. Then, as your business grows, you can phase in the tactics that have higher price tags. For example, let's say you'd like to advertise in several national magazines, but don't have the budget. You could contact the publications to find out if they rent their circulation lists, and do select mailings to the readers of just one or two. Other alternatives would be to target those national publications with a PR campaign or, if any of the publications offer regional editions, undertake your campaign with small-space ads in just one publication on a regional basis to start.

■ **Schedule Deadlines**

After all five sections of your sales and marketing plan are complete, take the most important step of all. Schedule and record the dates on which you'll take action to guarantee you'll stay on track. Plot the activities required to execute your plan using your contact management software, spreadsheet program, or a planning calendar. Note the dates on which in-house production must begin for projects such as broadcast fax newsletters and Web page updates. For instance, if you plan to broadcast fax a one- or two-page newsletter on August first, you might schedule production to begin July fifteenth, so you can give yourself about one week to assemble the content and another during which you'll find an hour or two to adjust the layout.

■ **Evaluate Your Plan Frequently**

Keep your schedule up to date, and modify it as your business and strategies evolve in response to alterations in your market or changes in the products or services you offer. Monitor the success of your sales and marketing program on an ongoing basis. If your program isn't working, quickly change or eliminate the ineffective strategies and adopt new ones. One of the biggest mistakes new home business owners make is to continue following a path long after it has stopped being productive. Evaluate the results of your program at least once per quarter in order to meet your goals. And rely on your written sales and marketing plan. You'll find it's a vital tool for measuring performance and a handy guide that will keep you on track.

CHECKLIST

✓ Create a five-section sales and marketing plan as follows:

- An overview of your competition, position in the market, specific challenges your business faces, and its unique niche and benefits.
- A target audience profile.
- A list of measurable goals and deadlines.
- A strategy section that details your sales and marketing strategies and the tactics you'll employ to reach your goals.
- A marketing budget.

✓ Review and edit your plan until it includes activities you can comfortably handle along with the day-to-day operation of your home-based business. Can you carry out the plan within your present budget? If not, assign alternate tactics to achieve your goals.

✓ Plan the steps you'll take to execute the tactics. Plot a schedule and record the dates on which you'll take action using contact management software, a planning calendar, or a spreadsheet program.

✓ Evaluate and measure the results of your sales and marketing program at least quarterly. Adjust your plan to take advantage of the most successful strategies and tactics, and continually modify or eliminate the ones that fall short.

TWENTY-THREE

Sound Like a Pro

Truth: The way your company "sounds" on the telephone can have a powerful impact on your bottom line.

■ ■ ■

Prospects will form instantaneous opinions about your home business based on two things—the way your company "looks" when they receive your materials, and the way it "sounds" the first time they contact you on the telephone. In chapter 5, we discussed the best ways to create a solid first impression with quality marketing materials. But did you know it's possible to positively affect the amount and type of work your company wins simply by fine-tuning the first impression prospects receive when they contact you on the telephone? With the proliferation of low-cost, high-quality telephone technology available and a little prior planning on your part, your home-based business can sound as professional as any major company.

CREATE A SOUND IMAGE

In 1998, home businesses spent nearly $45 billion dollars on telephone services alone, according to IDC. And for good reason. Communication is the lifeblood of every home business, and your telephone line is your most basic, yet multifunctional, tool.

■ Add Dedicated Lines

Ideally, you'll need at least two dedicated phone lines. Designate one as your principal telephone number for inbound calls, including your toll-free number, and use the second as a dedicated fax and modem line and for outbound calls. You can configure this in any number of ways depending upon your present equipment. Use your dedicated fax/modem line for outbound calls by plugging in a line splitter and a second telephone. Or if your fax machine has a telephone receiver, you can use it for outbound calls when the fax and modem are not in use. This will keep your main line free to receive calls from prospects and customers.

In some parts of the United States, you may choose to use either residential or business lines in your home office. However, most local telephone companies charge higher rates for service to business accounts. So unless you'll need Yellow Page listings, which are only available to business customers, it's to your advantage to add additional residential lines for your home-based business where permitted.

■ Answer Professionally

The way your telephone is answered can instantly communicate your level of professionalism or sabotage your company's ability to achieve its goals. Callers will make snap judgments about the nature and scope of work they'll entrust to your firm based on this important first impression. When you're in your home office and the telephone rings, do you answer simply with your name or "hello?" If so, you may be unwittingly communicating to callers that your business is quite small, thereby eroding your ability to win plum projects or clients.

The best way to answer your business line is with your company name first, followed by your own, such as "PC Troubleshooters, this is John Jones." This professional greeting lets callers know they've reached a place of business. By including your name in the greeting, you make callers comfortable by letting them know exactly who they're talking to, and your overall polish will also help to create a positive first impression. Always say your name last to make it easier to remember. For example, it's better to say, "This is John Jones," than "John Jones speaking."

Avoid letting children or other family members answer your business lines, even after hours. You should also resist the temptation to combine your personal family message with the one business prospects or clients hear. For many types of businesses, there's no reason to "hide" the fact that you work from home, and your customers may know where and how you work. But never relax your professionalism. Most clients or customers will expect you to keep your home life from taking over your business.

ADOPT SOUND TECHNOLOGY

Sometimes working from a home office can be a mixed blessing, particularly when background noise from children or pets intrudes during important telephone conversations. (There's more about children and the home office in chapter 29.) Nearly every home business owner I've met has at least one story of how a son returning from a soccer game with noisy friends, a loud neighbor, or a barking dog wrecked havoc during a critical call—and I'm no exception.

When my first book was published in the early nineties, I was interviewed by many broadcast and print media. Early one particular morning, I was giving a live interview by telephone from my home office to a raucous on-air team from a Boston radio station. Just as the interview got underway, a messenger arrived and began ringing the doorbell insistently. Instead of simply leaving the package, the messenger continued to ring, and then knock, throughout the entire ten-minute interview. At first, my ninety-pound dog, Brandy, gave out small woofs. But with the repeated ringing and knocking at the front door, he became increasingly agitated, and by the end of the ten minutes, he was hurling his body up against the steel-reinforced front door—barking and thudding, barking and thudding. Between the messenger's ringing and knocking and the big dog's frenzy, I barely heard a single question I was asked; I made my way through the interview by talking continuously—giving tips on home office success.

Fortunately, in the years since that experience, we've all benefited from the wider availability of technology that can help prevent such mishaps. Home office telephones by companies such as Panasonic often include mute buttons, and cordless telephones make it possible to take the phone with you to a quieter location in a pinch.

▪ Invest in a Headset

Home business owners who spend significant time on the telephone should invest in one of the newly affordable headsets, which attach easily to the telephone. Not only can they help prevent neck and back problems, many are available with noise-canceling microphones. So if you regularly work in an environment where random background noise intrudes on your telephone conversations, these mics can help filter it out and ensure it doesn't intrude on important conversations with prospects and customers. You can choose from a variety of models, including those that fit lightly over the ear, and cordless headsets that give you the freedom to move around your home office without restriction. Some also offer "clickless" mute switches, so you can inaudibly handle what would otherwise be noisy emergencies without interrupting your calls. When shopping for a headset, test models until you find the one with the best sound quality.

▪ Avoid Call Waiting

Local telephone companies nationwide offer a variety of services that can help you stay on top of your communications and project a big-company image. They also offer some services that are inappropriate for use on a business line, such as call waiting. The fact is, most people *hate* waiting. Don't you? Never use call waiting on a business line—it flies in the face of your efforts to put your customers or clients first. When you put a prospect or customer on hold to take another call, you're in effect telling them they're not important enough to maintain your entire focus for the length of a conversation. This type of behavior can erode customer satisfaction and communicate to prospects that winning their business is not your principal priority.

▪ Rely on Voicemail

Sometimes, home business owners with one telephone line or those who are on the telephone a great deal use call waiting because it eliminates busy signals. Voicemail from your local telephone company is always a better alternative to call waiting, because it offers you many of the benefits that larger companies expect from their phone systems. For individuals running home-based businesses, voicemail from the phone company is a terrific, low-cost alternative to adding the equipment in-house.

Local telephone companies have various names for voicemail, such as answer call, but most offer a fairly uniform set of features. With voicemail, there's never a busy signal, so your customers and prospects can leave messages even when you're on your line. You also have the option of setting up multiple mailboxes that enable prospects and customers to accomplish a great deal without having to reach you. Use your mailboxes to supply important product or service information, provide answers to frequently asked questions, and even take product orders. It's a good idea to script your outgoing messages for each mailbox. Record and rerecord your outgoing messages until they sound upbeat and professional.

If there are several people working in your home office, instead of voicemail from the phone company, consider a three-line telephone with multiple mailboxes and electronic answering. The Venture phones from Nortel Networks, for example, can connect up to eight workstations and let you transfer calls, communicate by intercom, and maintain individual phone directories.

When customers reach your voicemail or multiline telephone system with multiple mailboxes, they have no idea whether your business has one person or one hundred on staff, and most don't care, because their needs are immediately met. Depending upon your type of business, you may want to set up an arrangement that lets callers choose to reach a live person, such as an operator or answering service, and avoid "voicemail jail." No matter whether you use voicemail from your phone company or a state-of-the-art telephone system, your goals must be to create a big-company image and serve customers even when you're unavailable. Your company doesn't have to be big to sound smart.

CHECKLIST

✓ Make your business "sound" as professional as you are. Do you have at least one, preferably two, dedicated phone lines for your business? Be sure to arrange for "business" service if you need a listing in the Yellow Pages.

✓ When you answer your business lines, always use a professional greeting that includes an introduction of your company and yourself. Never allow family members to answer your business lines, even after hours, when calls may come in from clients or customers who want to leave messages or get information about your company.

✓ Use technology such as telephones with muting capabilities and headsets with noise-canceling microphones in situations where background noise is a problem.

✓ Increase your productivity and build your bottom line by getting the most from your telephone lines. Set up voicemail from your local telephone company or use a telephone answering system with multiple mailboxes. Use the mailboxes to provide information, answer questions, and even take product orders when you're unavailable.

TWENTY-FOUR

Polish Your Presentations

Truth: Effective presentations and seminars close sales and position you as an expert in your field.

■ ■ ■

Robin Gorman Newman, author of *How to Meet a Mensch in New York*, says she was "pretty horrified" the first time she had to speak in front of an audience. The president of Mensch Finders and self-styled "love coach" (whom I introduced in chapter 17) found it disquieting at first to make the transition from writing, which is a solitary task, to becoming a more public figure. It doesn't help that Newman lectures on a very personal subject—dating. Over time, she has learned to enjoy speaking in public and is energized by a positive response from an audience. Speaking fees have become a valuable source of revenue for her consulting firm, and appearances also generate new clients and book sales.

Many people find speaking to groups intimidating. There's even been a published report or two that reveal more people are afraid of public speaking than say they're afraid of death! But after about twenty years of making professional presentations to groups and helping others to succeed at it, I can promise you that no one (that I know of) has ever died from speaking in public, and it's actually an exhilarating experience. Whether you're trying to convince a group of investors to fall in line behind your latest and greatest idea, or speaking in front of twelve hundred of your peers at a convention, good presentation skills are powerful allies for motivating groups large and small.

KEYS FOR A SUCCESSFUL PRESENTATION

Presentations typically fall into two types: those that provide an opportunity to sell to a group, and seminars or workshops for the purpose of delivering content. Some home business owners provide both. Peter Sierck, the president of Environmental Testing and Technology, whom I introduced in chapter 17, speaks at major seminars to support his position as an expert in his field, and he has also created a special set of fee-based, three-day workshops for professionals in related fields on topics such as how to deal with mold problems in homes.

- **Offer Valuable Content**
Successful presentations are influenced by three factors. The first is the quality of your message. Before any presentation, learn as much about your audience as possible. This will help to ensure your talk is on target—not over their heads or below their knowledge level. It must be immediately apparent from the outset that what you say is of value. Ask yourself, "What is the audience hoping to gain from my talk?" and create a benefit-oriented presentation that provides clear and useful content. Even when making a sales presentation to a group, your focus must be on how what your company offers will benefit your audience members. Center your message on the benefits your prospects will achieve by accepting your proposed "solution" as the single best choice for their company.

- ## Follow a Logical Structure

The way your talk flows together, its structure, is the second factor that will strongly influence your presentation's success or failure. The structure must be logical, flowing from point A to point B easily and naturally, without digressions or omissions. It may be helpful to script your talk, though many speakers begin with a simple outline. Memorize and rehearse your presentation, then throw away the script. Never read from a canned speech—it's guaranteed to make the audience tune out and will undermine your image as an expert on your topic.

Anticipate the questions you'll receive and plan for audience interaction. Questions from the audience show they're engaged and interested, and are usually a sign your presentation is going well. Stony silence is most often an indication of the opposite—boredom, displeasure, and lack of involvement in the topic. The exception might be a group of business prospects who have solicited your presentation as a part of a competitive bid situation. They may be poker-faced and noncommittal so as not to show favoritism or "tip their hand."

- ## The Winning Formula

The third factor in your success, your presentation technique, is influenced by your personal style. The right formula is: *Great look + polished delivery = winning style*. The materials you choose can make or break the look of your presentation, and your ability to deliver your presentation without distracting mannerisms can rescue even ho-hum content.

Presentation Tools. In chapter 13, I advised you to use only high-quality tools and match them to the needs of your particular product or service and the size and type of audience to whom you'll be presenting. For presentations with a great look, it's also vital to select the type of presentation tools that best suit the environment in which they'll be used. Group presentations are not the place for intimate tools such as portfolios that have to be paged through individually or company brochures that must be read quietly to oneself.

Typically, your audience will be seated, though not necessarily captive. In many cases, they'll be able to simply leave if your visual presentation is dull, boring, or irrelevant to their needs. Contemporary presentation tools help ensure a great look that will keep them in their seats. Outdated tools such as flip charts and overheads can't possibly compete with the visual appeal and entertainment potential of computer-guided presentations that use a projector and screen, or the sound and motion of videotape displayed on monitors around a small room or on a large screen in an auditorium.

▪ Putting It All Together

Here's an example that demonstrates how your message, presentation structure, and style form the key components of a typical presentation.

Imagine you and a partner own a direct marketing agency, and you're making a presentation to the marketing department of a regional banking chain to propose a campaign to build customer use of debit cards. Your message (content) must provide reasonable solutions—a benefit-oriented description of the ways you will build debit card use. So you'll use appropriate language to demonstrate your grasp of direct marketing techniques, and you'll focus on the unique history and position of your banking prospect in the marketplace and how they will affect its ability to carry out an effective campaign.

The presentation is structured as follows: a description of the target audience; how you'll reach them; what you'll say to customers who receive the direct mail campaign; and why the solutions you propose will yield the highest possible customer response. The tools you select to present to this small, sophisticated marketing group must convey the key points of your presentation and attractively display samples of similar campaigns you've successfully conducted. So you choose a presentation tool, PowerPoint software, that allows you to combine static visuals with video. Your equipment includes a laptop, LCD projector, and portable screen.

When it comes to style, you and your partner deliver an up-beat, clear presentation, taking turns standing next to the screen. As the primary client contact, you open and close the presentation and cover select sections, while your partner, who's in charge of creative development and execution, presents the sections that relate directly to the unique approach you will take to motivate customers to use their debit cards. To close, both you and your partner take questions and participate in a discussion with your prospective clients.

From the above example, you can see how important it is that your content, structure, and style work together to create a positive presentation. Unfortunately, many presenters have difficulty with negative behaviors that detract from their success. To polish your own presentation technique, set up a videotape recorder and tape several rehearsals. You'll be amazed at how many potential problems you'll notice.

A MATTER OF STYLE

Over the past twenty years, I've categorized presentation style into eleven types. Ten are style-busters. Problem technique comes from inexperience and lack of guidance, and can usually be corrected quickly with training and practice. The first four style problems are caused by verbal distractions. As you watch your videotaped rehearsal, look for these verbal detractors.

- **Verbal Distractions**
Are you a "slow talker"? If you speak at an usually slow or halting rate, your audience will become bored and begin to pay more attention to your speech patterns than what you have to

say. The same holds true if you're a "low talker" who speaks quietly, looking down at the floor. This conveys shyness and makes the audience uncomfortable. Does your presentation go on endlessly with no beginning, middle, or end in sight? "Droners" are unsure when enough is enough. Many inexperienced presenters tend to be "repeaters," who say a single word like "um" or "well," or a phrase such as "by and large," over and over again. These four types of verbal distractions can torpedo your presentation. Fortunately, they're among the easiest to spot and can be cured almost immediately with additional practice.

▪ Destructive Behavior

Other presentation problems arise not because of *how* we speak, but because we say things that detract from otherwise valuable content. These next four destructive types are harder to spot on your videotape, so ask friends or business partners you trust to watch your video with you and indicate where you may be sliding into these problem areas.

No matter what happens before or during your presentation, absolutely, positively never become an "apologizer." If you must say something about a problem, make a joke or poke fun at it instead. An apology, particularly at the outset of your presentation, will destroy your credibility and sabotage your talk. Examples of apologies of the worst kind are: "I'm not an expert in this but . . ." or "I was hoping to have more video to show you today but . . ." You must also be careful not to come across as a "double talker" or "show-off." If you present many unsubstantiated facts or overpromise, you'll be considered a double talker whose promises are probably too good to be true. A show-off tends to rely on too few facts, putting more emphasis on visual bells and whistles than on substance. And then there's the "techie," who may overwhelm his or her audience with minutiae and too many in-depth facts and industry jargon.

Probably the easiest presentation problems to spot stem from physical characteristics. The "stiff" hides behind a podium with hands folded, barely moving, and may even read from a script. This boring and entirely noninteractive presentation style can make an audience run for the door. The "twitcher" physically acts out his or her nervousness by grinning, grimacing, and making repetitious gestures, such as swaying from one foot to the other or repeatedly thumping the podium.

▪ Straight Shooters

Top presenters are "straight shooters." They use clear, direct language and move around the room or back and forth on the stage in front of the audience instead of standing stiffly behind a podium. Terrific presenters make eye contact with the audience, use natural and animated body movement, and handle their presentation tools with ease. They're comfortable to listen to and fun to watch, because they engage the audience and make each person feel as if he or she is being spoken to directly.

Look critically at your rehearsal video. Do you see signs of any problem presentation styles? The truth is, once you're aware of them, you can fix such problems easily and painlessly. Just keep practicing until the person you see on the screen reminds you of a polished presenter—perhaps a speaker you admire.

▪ Use a Leave-Behind

After a seminar or workshop, always give your audience something to take back to their homes or offices that summarizes the presentation or its key points and provides at least one paragraph of background on you and your company. If your presentation is part of a sales process, your "leave-behind" takes on even greater importance because it must provide a lasting reminder of the quality and content of your presentation. In a competitive situation, your presentation may be one among a half dozen your prospects will sit through in the course of just several days. By the end of that process, many of the presentations will run together in your prospects' minds, so make your leave-behind a comprehensive selling tool that can stand on its own.

CHECKLIST

✓ To create a winning presentation, concentrate on three areas: your message, presentation structure, and style. Write a script or outline the content of your talk to make it benefit-oriented. Decide what your audience wants to take away from your presentation, then focus the content to meet their specific needs. Make certain your talk is on the right knowledge level, not too elementary or over their heads.

✓ Structure your seminar or sales presentation so it flows logically from one point to the next. Make sure it has a beginning, middle, and end, with time allotted for interaction throughout or at specified points.

✓ Choose presentation tools that match the needs of your own type of product or service, the size of the audience, and the environment in which you'll be making your presentation. Use contemporary tools that are visually engaging to keep your audience focused on you and your message.

✓ Videotape several rehearsals and critique your performance. Look for any of the ten style-busters outlined in this chapter. Watch for verbal and physical habits that detract from your presentation and any other style problems, such as a tendency to get bogged down in technical details or to over-promise, that can derail otherwise solid content. Practice and retape your presentation until you have eliminated these problems, and your presentation style is as professional as you are.

TWENTY-FIVE

Build Strategic Partnerships

Truth: Teaming is the new survival strategy for home-based businesses.

■ ■ ■

Since the early nineties, journalists and researchers have been asking the question, What has fueled the dramatic rise in the number of home businesses in America? The answer is clear. The rise is due to the availability of low-cost technology and Americans' desire for more meaningful lifestyles. On the heels of downsizing, or "right sizing" as it's often been called, we're no longer content to leave our fate in the hands of major employers. So, many of us have chosen to become self-employed. Entrepreneurism is one of our most characteristically American traits. But none of this would have been possible without the PCs, fax machines, and other low-cost office equipment that we now often take for granted. Thirty years ago, an assembly-line worker in a factory anywhere in this country had few options. He or she could certainly not have quit factory life on Monday to set up a fully equipped home office as a consultant on Tuesday.

The good news is that workers of all types, knowledge workers and contractors and artisans alike, can now choose to go it alone. And that's the problem too. So many millions of home business owners and millions more small business operators are jumping into the marketplace, there's tremendous competition in every market niche. This leaves home-based business owners at a disadvantage in several ways: our businesses are less visible; we offer a narrower range of skills or services than larger firms; and we're limited by the amount we can accomplish in any given day, week, or month.

THE TEAM ADVANTAGE

This makes strategic partnering, or teaming, a crucial survival strategy for home business owners. Not an entirely new concept, strategic partnering is going on in Fortune 500 companies everywhere as they form alliances with other businesses and individuals who help them reach their goals. Even companies with tens of thousands of workers are no longer content to be limited to only those they can directly employ. In this chapter, I'll describe at least eight ways in which strategic partnering can help you achieve greater success.

▪ I. Increase Your Income

As an individual, you're limited to what you can charge for your own output or the number of units you can produce. Many home business owners charge for their services on an hourly basis. Consultants, copywriters, repairmen, artists, and many others, when working alone, are limited to what the market will bear when it comes to their hourly rates. However, when an art director teams with a copywriter, their strategic partnership allows them to bill as a unit for completed projects, which can have a profound effect on their annual income.

Many types of home businesses at first glance seemed limited to the time and talents of their founders. Take word processing, for example. Gail Klotz is president of the Home Office, a tape transcription service that she has run for sixteen years. Just five years ago, Klotz realized that in order to grow her business, she would need to spend more time on marketing and less on execution of transcription projects. So she began to team with independent contractors. Within the first two years of using independent transcribers to support her company's workload, Klotz doubled her income.

Today, her business is busier than ever. She uses a total of six transcribers and has plans to add more to take on a lucrative new contract. Klotz pays the independent contractors half of her per page transcription price, and she views each of them as individual profit centers. For Klotz, strategic partnering has proven a viable way to grow her business and dramatically increase her income. Her greatest present challenge is managing her team of transcribers, and she's considering adding more software and automation to help her track jobs and deadlines.

▪ 2. Gain a Competitive Advantage

Along with the skyrocketing numbers of small and home-based businesses, competition has increased in every field. If you started your business five years ago, chances are you had three or four competitors in your market niche. Today you may have thirty, and five years from now you could have three hundred. Teaming or partnering gives you a competitive advantage because, with a flexible set of relationships, you can fill varied requirements for your clients.

Suppose you're out to win a major contract with a large corporation. By teaming with a group of individuals with complementary skills, you can form a virtual corporation to pitch and win your contract. The team can remain together over time or disband, perhaps working together again in a variety of configurations to meet a host of different needs. Businesses with traditional employer/employee structures cannot transform themselves as rapidly. You'll also have another advantage if you team with highly expert and well-qualified senior individuals, particularly if you compete directly with companies that have traditional employee hierarchies. Their teams will consist of a larger number of junior-level employees, while your virtual corporation can consist of senior people who are chosen for their specific expertise.

Often, home business owners who partner with a particular individual over time have a competitive advantage too. Francis Chamberlain is a media consultant and writer who regularly partners with designer Nancy Mygatt, president of Mygatt Design Concepts. From their home offices in Washington, Connecticut, Chamberlain and Mygatt partner to handle complete creative projects from start to finish. Individually, each of them can only perform a part of the process—Chamberlain can write a newsletter, for example, and Mygatt can handle the design—but together they take on larger projects and ensure their clients a complete turnkey operation.

The team has been working together for approximately three years and now has six or seven steady clients. Plus, new clients come in regularly, and with much less effort than when each partner was selling on her own. Prospects may call on one of them individually, but when the other team member is needed, she readily takes her part. Chamberlain feels clients are impressed by the way she and her teammate work closely together but are not a traditional agency, with its standard overhead and markup costs. Clients believe they will get the same service that they might from a bigger company without higher rates.

▪ 3. Reduce Your Nonbillable Sales Hours

Most new home business owners spend approximately 40 to 60 percent of their time in sales and marketing. As you grow your business, you can reduce this to approximately 35 to 40 percent. Now suppose you partner with another individual to form a single team or unit. Instead of each team member spending 40 percent of his or her time in sales and marketing, each of you can reduce the amount of time you spend, say to about 20 percent, and split the duties evenly. Or one of you can become principally responsible for all sales and marketing—preferably the partner who enjoys and excels in both areas. Collectively, the same number of hours will be spent in sales and marketing, but now the duties will be shared. Best of all, working together, you may be able to dream up new or more innovative ways to market your partnership.

▪ 4. Relieve Your Isolation

We are always hearing about how lonely it is to work at home by oneself. The truth is, many home business owners think it's terrific—they prefer to operate without interruption or interaction that they may find distracting and stressful. As a former corporate executive, I confess that the conversation around the "water cooler" was often more of a time-waster than a stressbuster. Nevertheless, for many home business owners, constant isolation is less than ideal. (More about this in chapter 30.) Teaming offers pleasant relief from the problem.

When you and a partner work on a project from your own offices, the interaction involved in planning and execution can be energizing. And for extroverts, who draw energy from processing aloud or through interaction with others, this synergy of ideas can actually bring a renewal of spirit and a new kind of enjoyment to working from home. Chamberlain and Mygatt, for example, live several miles apart and often meet for coffee halfway or go to each other's homes when face-to-face interaction is required for their work. In many cases, strategic partnerships flourish thanks to communication by fax, e-mail, and telephone, particularly when the partners are out-of-state.

▪ 5. Grow Your Business

What happens when a business consultant in Los Angeles teams with practices in Chicago and Fort Lauderdale? They can share resources and knowledge, plus create a national image for their combined firms. This marketing partnership can also lay the groundwork for creation of a single, larger business.

Most any form of strategic partnering will help you grow your business. Your first step is to evaluate your short- and long-term goals. What vision do you have for your company? Are you planning to remain home-based or would you like to grow a Fortune 500 firm? The type of business you own, and the products or services you provide, will also dictate the best ways to partner. For businesses that require hands-on work, such as the transcription company mentioned above or general contracting businesses, teaming with independent contractors can be a great way to free up your time for marketing, management, and working one-on-one with clients or customers.

■ 6. Provide Additional Services

Teaming with businesses or individuals that provide complementary services can allow you to expand your customer base. For example, when an interior designer teams with a remodeling contractor, each gains a whole universe of new prospects and access to a greater number of referral clients.

What types of businesses could you partner with to get greater access to your target audience? Don't confine your partnership opportunities exclusively to other home-based or small businesses. Consider partnering with major corporations, provided you market to the same type of target audience. Associations, credit card companies, even long-distance carriers have what are called "affinity programs." That means they pull together a group of products and services that can enhance the value of their own, and offer them bundled together to their customers.

Take a look at the next credit card offer you receive in the mail. In addition to credit, you'll see card membership includes a whole variety of other services, from accident insurance and reduced rates on rental cars to travel planning. A home business owner that makes Web development software for small businesses, for example, might develop a strategic marketing partnership with a small business association to add value for their members. The membership would be offered the software, and the association would take a percentage of the income generated.

▪ 7. Gain Input from Experienced Partners

Suppose you were the Web development software company mentioned above. By forming a strategic partnership with a small business association, you'd do more than increase sales. You would gain input from partners experienced in marketing to your target audience. They could offer guidance on the type of approach that worked best with their members and would want to approve the marketing pieces you planned to mail. This would greatly reduce the chances of your marketing efforts falling flat. By allying yourself with strategic partners who have a vested interest in your success and the experience to help you mold your marketing approach, you can expect a higher return more quickly on your marketing efforts.

▪ 8. Reduce Your Marketing Costs

If you've been in business a while, you're probably aware of how much it costs to launch a new product or a new product line for an existing business. For those of us who don't have $5 or $10 million or more lying around, strategic partnering makes a lot of sense. Think about how much the Web development software inventor above would save by piggybacking his product launch on the existing marketing program of a major advertiser. Without the partnership, he or she would have to test market the product, try numerous offers to figure out what worked best, build an enormous prospect list, or even coordinate and oversee a massive national direct marketing campaign. But thanks to the strategic partnership, all the inventor has to do is print enough marketing pieces for each mailing, if individual pieces are required, and of course have a high-quality product on hand in sufficient quantity to fill sales.

Strategic partnering is a terrific way to cut the cost of testing a new product with your audience. Let's say you create beautiful, hand-painted coffee mugs. You get the idea to create a line of mugs with handles in the shape of parrots. You test the product at craft shows, where the mugs sell moderately well, but you're sure that bird enthusiasts would be a great target market for the new line. So you contact an association for exotic bird owners and convince them to use your mugs in their catalog or as a special premium. That way you test the market with minimal investment, because the association provides the marketing vehicle and the ready audience. Get the idea?

You can also partner to share marketing costs with your local team members. Chamberlain and Mygatt have just begun to advertise their writing and design services jointly, and are designing a Web site together to generate more color catalog and magazine work.

Once you decide to set up a team relationship or strategic partnership, it's a good idea to put the parameters of your relationship in writing. You want to be certain everyone understands what's expected of them and is committed to living up to their agreements. Invest some time in negotiating, planning, and formalizing your partnership relationships, and your efforts will be well rewarded.

CHECKLIST

✓ Evaluate your company's growth goals to determine what types of strategic partnerships or team relationships will help get you where you want to go. Also consider how new relationships will affect the way you like to work. How will your job responsibilities change? If you choose to work with a number of independent contractors to take over hands-on work that you presently perform on your own, how will you feel about spending more time in marketing and management, and less producing the work?

✓ Identify the types of businesses with which you could develop strategic partnerships to reach your target audience. Look for companies or individuals that offer complementary services.

✓ Set up teams or strategic partnerships that give you a competitive advantage, enable you to provide additional services, or help reduce the cost of bringing your product to the target audience. Then formalize your plans in writing so there can be no problems or misunderstandings down the road.

TWENTY-SIX

Ensure Customer Satisfaction

Truth: Dissatisfied customers rarely complain; they just go someplace else.

• • •

In the next few years, your business will change in response to your customers' needs in ways you may not even imagine today. Remember Phil Hagen from chapter 18? He started a Web site, www.dcregistry.com, and within several years he ended up marketing a program for online classified advertising, called e-Classifieds. The product was created because he and other "Webpreneurs" needed help but couldn't find a program like it anywhere else. By responding to his customers, Hagen created a product that would satisfy their requirements and, in the process, significantly increased his financial success.

Responding to clients' needs also led to increased success for Gail Klotz, president of the transcription service, the Home Office, that I mentioned in the last chapter. Swamped with work and absolutely committed to meeting her clients' deadlines, she made the decision to team with independent contractors to handle the workload. Klotz retained her commitment to customer satisfaction and freed up a portion of her time to deal with existing accounts and acquire new ones. As a result, her business has doubled in size.

HOME-BASED ADVANTAGES

When it comes to customer satisfaction, your home business has several major advantages over larger companies. The most dramatic is the speed at which you can respond to the changing needs of your market. There are no committees, corporate divisions, or management levels to go through. You can spot a need and fill it by altering your product, creating a new one, or restructuring the way your services are offered—all in a fraction of the time it would take a larger competitor.

▪ You Can Quickly Resolve Complaints

A second advantage is your ability to instantly resolve customers' complaints or problems. When a customer has a problem with a company that has fifty employees, or fifty thousand for that matter, what chance has he got of actually speaking to someone with the ability to immediately rectify the problem and make amends? Clients and customers like working with home business owners because they have one-on-one access to "the boss." Even home businesses with several owners and employees retain this advantage because most or all individuals are empowered to make on the spot decisions when it comes to handling unhappy clients or customers.

▪ You Get Direct Feedback

Home business owners also benefit from direct customer feedback. You don't have to wait for input from a sales department or customer service division to find out which way the wind blows. The fact is, you may only hear from a small percentage of unhappy customers and an even tinier percentage of those who are delighted with your company or your work. According to the Society of Consumer Affairs Professionals in Business (SOCAP), only about one-third of dissatisfied customers ever complain. Most rarely speak out, they simply move on. And SOCAP's research shows that negative word of mouth is spread *and believed* at twice the rate of positive word of mouth.

Quality products and services are expected at most price levels. Do you truly know how your customer or client base feels about the level of quality you offer? Do you meet their expectations? The key to gaining the greatest understanding of customer satisfaction is to develop basic tools for getting feedback. Mail comment cards or evaluation forms regularly, send letters asking for feedback (as well as referrals), make your Web site interactive, and actively solicit testimonial letters from happy clients or customers. It costs five times more to win customers than to keep them, according to SOCAP, and actively soliciting customer input improves the chances of repeat business.

▪ You Get to Know Your Customers

One more advantage you have as a home-based business owner—and someone committed to customer satisfaction—is the privilege of getting to know most of your clients and customers well. Good service is a marketing tool that builds positive word of mouth. No one likes being treated as if they are simply a number or a faceless account that represents just so much revenue. That's how customers or clients of many major businesses are made to feel, and it's one good reason they'll often choose a more personal relationship with the head of a smaller organization like yours.

If yours is the type of business that only works with a handful of clients at any one time, the relationships you develop will be based as much on friendship and mutual respect as on your company's ability to get the job done. For home-based businesses with large numbers of customers, including those selling products with lower price points, making customers feel special and valued as individuals is still important. They'll come back to you time and again if you develop methods and materials that treat each customer according to his or her individual needs.

▪ You Can Respond Immediately

Home business owners can go the extra mile. Here's a true story. On a beautiful Sunday afternoon over a year ago, our neighbor's seemingly healthy eight-story-tall oak tree came crashing down on our house. Part of the roof was crushed and a large limb smashed through the first-floor dining room window, jutting about seven feet into the room. No one was hurt, but we had to do something immediately about the part of the tree that was preventing us from boarding up and securing the dining room window for the night.

I made several calls to tree services and got recordings. This was to be expected, since it was now nearly Sunday evening. But one fellow picked up the call on his cellular phone, and within minutes he and his wife and children pulled up in front of our house. They'd been on their way to Sunday dinner when my call came in. Over my protestations, the fellow sent his family on without him and called his team members. Soon, by flashlight, he and two other men put supports under the trunk of the enormous tree, which still rested on top of our house, severed the protruding limb, and secured the dining room window. The next day he returned with a full tree removal crew to finish the job.

We were impressed and grateful—and you can bet everyone on our street knew how that fellow's company had come through for us. Since all our neighbors have wooded lots with mature trees, his tremendous dedication to customer service has resulted in numerous major tree removal jobs for his home-based business. And he's made customers for life.

BE A PROBLEM SOLVER

While home business owners enjoy several significant customer service advantages over larger companies, each comes with business and professional challenges.

- **Respond Quickly**

It's no secret that time is your most precious commodity, and it's time that can get in the way of ensuring customer satisfaction. For home business owners, particularly those in consumer service businesses, just returning telephone calls in a timely manner can pose a tremendous challenge. But if you don't return calls within at least twenty-four hours, you'll lose business and damage your company image. A good solution is to rely on technology to help you stay in touch.

One local remodeling contractor gives each of his customers his cell phone number to use at any time. As he moves from jobsite to jobsite supervising work and providing estimates, customers with questions or concerns can instantly reach him. Even though remodeling can be stressful for most homeowners, he gets few angry or panic-stricken calls because customers can reach him immediately for answers. Voicemail, answering machines, pagers, and cellular phones all facilitate instant communication with your customers, but they don't necessarily increase satisfaction unless customers have a chance to speak with a real person when they need help the most.

- **Don't Take It Personally**

Being the first to hear customer criticism and general feedback is a double-edged sword. You can respond to your customers' changing needs quickly and insightfully and handle complaints directly. But here's the problem. As a business owner, everything that happens, good or bad, may have a more personal tinge to it. When you were employed by someone else and a customer or client was dissatisfied with the company's services or you lost an account, you probably took it with a grain of salt. But now, negative feedback or, at worst, being fired by a client feels like a personal defeat, a stab at your integrity, ability, and competence.

Your *number one challenge* is to learn to distance yourself from this type of reaction. If you take negatives too personally, you become angry or withdrawn, thereby losing the objectivity necessary to reasonably resolve conflicts. Remember the old maxim, The customer is always right. It's your job to look objectively at the input you receive, whether negative or positive. When a customer or client presents you with a problem, apologize quickly and make amends. That means to offer some sort of restitution, replacement, or special gift. Which brings us to the next challenge. . . .

▪ Guarantees and Liability

Every company must offer guarantees and stand behind what they sell, don't you agree? Of course, your head tells you this is absolutely true, but when restitution comes out of your own pocket it's sometimes another matter. What specific guarantees does your company offer? Are they in writing? By law, if you sell a product via direct mail you must have a written return policy. But what if you supply a highly sophisticated service to just three or four principal clients? Your work agreement should also be spelled out in writing and signed by both parties.

No matter what type of home-based business you're in, liability insurance is a good idea. Say you're a deck builder and you've just completed a large job on a new home. At the housewarming party, a railing on the deck comes loose and several guests are injured. Without liability insurance, your entire business and personal belongings could be at risk. Increasingly, major insurers are offering low-cost liability insurance, for as little as about two hundred dollars a year, as a part of their business policies. In most cases, however, making amends involves relatively minor expenditures. Most often, conflict resolution requires open communication with a genuine willingness to hear and understand the customer or client's point of view.

■ Customer Feedback

How do you measure customer or client satisfaction? If you sell a product, customer comment cards are a terrific way to get feedback and basic data on your customer base. The next time you buy any consumer or business product, such as a tape player, fax machine, or printer, take a good look at the manufacturer's registration card. You'll notice it asks for helpful demographic data and offers some sort of reward in return, such as a promise to notify you of upgrades or speedy warranty verification. Use these examples as models to design your own comment card, and use it religiously. Enclose a card with every product sold, and use the ones that are returned to help expand your understanding of your customers and build a database for testing additional offers.

Where comment cards are inappropriate, letters and surveys can be used to gain more detailed responses. For example, one custom homebuilder sends a two-page survey letter following the completion of every project. He knows that after spending months or years working with an individual or couple, a written questionnaire will give them the opportunity to supply candid feedback. More often than not, he receives glowing comments that he can use (by permission) in his marketing materials.

Sometimes customer feedback will spark a terrific new idea for your business. Before you spend lots of money to develop and launch it, try using other methods to gain broader customer input. Use informal focus groups with customers or prospects to explore your new concept. If you have a Web site, use it interactively to get feedback on the idea. You may even be able to test market the concept online for a minimal cost.

■ Reward Your Customers

Have you ever had dinner at a restaurant and then been pleasantly surprised to receive free dessert as a thank-you? Or have you ever received a special thank-you gift in the mail when you ordered from a major catalog? If so, your pleasant, memorable surprise was courtesy of an effective customer rewards program. Think of how you can say "thank you" to your own customers or clients in a way that will be surprising or fun. An unexpected thank-you will be more highly regarded than a gift or restitution you must offer in order to make amends or solve a problem. So why wait?

CHECKLIST

✓ How long does it take you to return calls from customers or prospects? If it's more than twenty-four hours, you're putting your business reputation and long-range success at risk. Evaluate the ways technology can help you improve customer service. Cellular telephones, pagers, voicemail—even answering services—can help you make the most of your time while remaining accessible to your customer or client base.

✓ Never take negative feedback personally. Listen to criticism objectively. If there's been an error or lapse in service or product quality, apologize briefly and make amends by offering restitution, replacement, or a promise of renewed effort.

✓ What promises or guarantees does your company make? Put your guarantees and agreements in writing, and explore the benefits of business liability insurance. On a day-to-day basis, this type of insurance may never be needed, but should a disaster happen, you'll be protected.

✓ Institute regular programs to measure customer or client satisfaction. Depending on your type of business, you may want to design a comment card or formulate a survey letter. Use ongoing communications, such as your Web page or electronic newsletter, to gather feedback on new concepts or offerings.

✓ Look for surprising ways to reward customers or clients. Your customer rewards program need not be expensive. A small thank-you goes a long way toward showing customers you value their business.

TWENTY-SEVEN

Take On International Markets

Truth: International markets fuel growth for many home businesses with less than a million dollars in sales.

■ ■ ■

When Rob Wilkinson and his partner, Colleen Chartier, began photographing public art projects in Seattle, Washington, back in 1982, they didn't plan to build an international company. But today their firm, ART on FILE, Inc., sells 35mm slides and digital CD-ROMs of contemporary art, architecture, and design to colleges and universities worldwide. Scenically located in a small section of downtown Seattle that's surrounded on three sides by water, their studio has been remodeled and converted from what was once a garage, and sits adjacent to a beautifully landscaped pond behind Wilkinson's 1920s-style home. Back in the early 1980s, while photographing in Seattle, the partners found colleges and universities were very interested in their work. That led to a National Endowment for the Arts grant, according to Wilkinson, that allowed them to travel and do photography under the auspices of the Visual Resource Association.

Today, the pair continues to travel overseas and within the United States to photograph and write about their subjects.

Wilkinson's four-prong marketing strategy, including advertising, PR, a catalog, and a Web site, has produced significant results for this home-based business. International sales from the United Kingdom, Europe, China, and Australia constitute a significant source of revenue for ART on FILE, which actively targets prospects overseas. His strategy includes placing advertising and public relations in a quarterly bulletin of the Visual Resource Association, which reaches most professional media librarians. For direct sales, ART on FILE has historically offered a black-and-white catalog to universities and colleges. But that is currently being replaced by the company's Web site, www.artonfile.com. Wilkinson believes the site gives his company a better opportunity to affordably showcase and market all of ART on FILE's products online.

Wilkinson promotes the company's Web site in his advertising in the quarterly bulletin, with special postcard mailings to his database, and through standard online promotional devices including listings with search engines. Long before the Web site, Wilkinson and his partner had built a bridge to the United Kingdom through development of a marketing relationship with the Public Art Development Trust, a London-based organization that's supported by grants. The trust assists Wilkinson and Chartier in doing research and coordinating trips in Europe and the United Kingdom. They also distribute joint catalogs, and market on behalf of ART on FILE.

Wilkinson and Chartier's story illustrates how today's home business owners are successfully adding international components to their marketing programs. Time and again, you'll see the two principal strategies include: establishing a relationship with a business or individual overseas; and developing a Web presence that makes products and services available worldwide.

Sue Redmore's new business provides another terrific example. After fifteen years working in marketing communications and channel marketing positions in the high-tech industry in Europe and North America, Redmore founded DragonFire Marketing and Business Communications in Santa Cruz, California. Working from a home office, Redmore provides on- and off-site consulting to Silicon Valley companies and offers services in partnership with Berkeley PR International, a pan-European PR agency based in the United Kingdom. Redmore formed this alliance because she found many high-tech companies wanted to expand into Europe but didn't know how to find distributors or get in touch with journalists there. DragonFire Marketing and Berkeley PR offer their services in tandem and refer business back and forth. As a part of this partnership, Redmore handles the PR services in the United States for U.K. companies who wish to expand into this country, and she establishes contacts with high-tech companies who want to expand into the European market for Berkeley. Both companies, DragonFire and Berkeley PR, have Web sites that target the U.S. and U.K. markets.

INTERNATIONAL TRADE RESOURCES

If you're new to international sales, your first step should be to contact the Trade Information Center (TIC) at the U.S. Department of Commerce. This is a comprehensive resource on all federal government export assistance programs, coordinating the services of nineteen different federal agencies. You may speak to an international trade specialist on the TIC's toll-free line, 800-USA-TRADE, where you can get advice on how to locate and use government programs, sources for general market information, and basic export counseling. You can also request a package of information including recommended publications to guide you through export transactions; where to find trade leads and financing for exporting; and sources for market research and country information.

▪ Search the Web

There are online resources, too, that can help you bridge the culture gaps. Michigan State University's Center for International Business Education and Research provides a comprehensive list of links to international business resources on the Web. Visitors to its site (http://ciber.bus.msu.edu/busres.htm) will find information on specific countries and regions, international conferences, trade shows and business events, and trade laws, as well as links to sites for sourcing trade leads. A click on links to resources on Asia and Oceania, for example, provides a description of more than fifty Web sites with articles and information on places including Japan, China, and India.

Inc. magazine's online guide to international business (www.inc.com/international), offers a "real questions, real answers" directory that includes advice on how to find sales agents in foreign countries. There are data and advice on export issues for eighty countries, country-by-country Web links, and an online bulletin board to post partnering opportunities.

Another way to make contacts overseas is to search the Web for foreign-based companies that offer similar or complementary services to yours with which you can develop and build relationships over time just as Sue Redmore did. You can also visit the Trade Information Center's Web site at www.ita.doc.gov/tic/ for answers to frequently asked questions concerning international trade. While there, investigate the site's information on trade missions to overseas markets, where you can meet with potential distributors and buyers.

▪ Establish Local Contacts

Perhaps you're not ready to join trade missions to Japan or parts of Europe just yet. Why not join international trade and government organizations in your area and attend their events? You can also register for their news and e-mail discussion groups to build leads and generate awareness for your home-based business. For example, Redmore has developed relationships with the Invest in Britain division of the British consulate, located in San Francisco, and other locally-based European trade organizations, which provide excellent contacts and advice for building her business.

■ Make Friends Overseas

Overseas connections don't have to be formal business partnerships. Sometimes a friend in a foreign country can give you the kind of insightful information you need to prevent you from making costly mistakes. That was the case for Caroline Keating, president of Caroline's Closets of Santa Monica, California. Caroline's Closets is a home-based business that runs a bilingual e-commerce site selling American vintage clothing exclusively via the Web. Keating started the business right out of UCLA, where she studied Japanese. During trips to Japan, Keating saw groups of young people dressed entirely in American clothes from the 1950s, and discovered the Japanese have a keen interest in American vintage clothing. As a result, her company's Web site, www.carolinesclosets.com, has been created in two versions—English and Japanese.

By a stroke of luck, Keating has a Japanese friend who supplied vital information on the way the Japanese prefer to make purchases online. Keating's friend advised her not to attempt to take credit card orders on the Web site, because he believes the Japanese are not yet confident the Web is a secure environment. Consequently, Keating is gearing up to take orders from the Japanese market by formulating an order form that visitors to the Japanese site can print out, then fax back with their credit card numbers. It's this kind of grass-roots advice from an individual or business partner based in your overseas market that can ensure a lack of cultural information doesn't stand in your way.

Think of ways you can expand your home-based business through international sales. Then start slowly, building your

Web content, knowledge of the export process, and contacts in foreign markets over time.

CHECKLIST

✓ Start by doing some homework on basic export practices with help from the Trade Information Center at the Department of Commerce (800-USA-TRADE) and online resources. Research each of the countries in which you plan to build sales, and become familiar with their local customs and buying preferences.

✓ Join international trade organizations in your area. Become a part of their online discussion groups to learn more about international sales and to build relationships.

✓ Set up and maintain a Web site that targets your overseas customers and communicates the specific benefits your products and services provide. Don't forget to take into account how you'll handle processing and fulfillment of overseas orders.

✓ Make contacts overseas via the Web, membership in international organizations, or trade missions sponsored by your state or the federal government.

TWENTY-EIGHT

Work Where and How You Choose

Truth: From the beach to your own backyard, your "office" can be anywhere you like to work.

■ ■ ■

This chapter is about having the freedom to live and work in the style that suits you best. The arrival of the information age means we no longer have to go where the work is. The work comes to us—or with us—as millions of telecommuters and home business owners prove every day. Many found that being confined to a desk in an office building turned work they loved into drudgery and could even result in ill health. Now, for the one-third of all American workers who do at least some of their work from home, the home office is a comfortable environment in which to get the job done. However, even a spacious home office can seem confining after a while if you spend all your work hours there.

TRY A CHANGE OF SCENE

Home business owners have an average fifty-hour work week. For contractors, consultants, salespeople, and many others who must leave home to meet with clients or work in the field, a few hours spent quietly at their desks may be a welcome respite. But for many others, such as writers and Web designers, a change of scene—even if it's a move to the living room couch—can be energizing. Mountain retreats, woodland hideaways, garden paths, suburban poolsides, and city cafés have all become workplaces thanks to portable technology. And millions of home workers are getting out and enjoying their new work- and lifestyles.

As you read this, Sue Cross may be meeting a tight deadline— from the deck of her sailboat. Cross is president of Cross Reference, a fifteen-year-old multimedia and technical writing and documentation business based in Oak Park, California. She uses a Macintosh PowerBook with a solar panel to work full days while sailing around the Channel Islands of California. She says she finds the surroundings inspirational, and the extended peace and quiet helpful when dealing with sticky creative issues. With the solar panel, Cross says she gets four to five hours of computing time per lithium ion battery. If she needs more, she plugs into a cigarette lighter socket on the boat.

I told you a bit about Cross in chapter 5, and the on-location work she is doing for the U.S. Park Service with the help of her notebook computer and a digital camera. So it's not surprising that Cross takes her computer when she goes camping in the mountains. Once, while sitting at a picnic table working, a hummingbird became interested in what she was doing. It hovered around her shoulder, probably because it was interested in her red cap, though Cross jokes, "I think he was reading my manuscript." It's this love of nature and the outdoors that has led to her long-term goal—to cruise on the sailboat permanently and maintain her business. Cross is waiting for technology to catch up with her dreams and for someone to produce a cellular modem that will work when she's far from land.

▪ Escape Cramped Quarters

No matter how wonderfully designed and equipped a home office may be, when two people work there, it can sometimes feel a bit crowded. Linda Formichelli was working in her home office in Attleboro, Massachusetts, for two years before her husband, W. Eric Martin, joined her there. Both are freelance writers who sometimes collaborate by editing each other's work. The couple shares an office with two computers, but Linda says usually one of them is working somewhere else in the house using an old PowerBook, which they bought second-hand several years ago. Formichelli believes it recharges them to go somewhere different, because in their home office they're always distracted by the telephone and e-mail. For a change of pace, three or four times a week they pack up their portable computer, folders, and decaf teabags and head to their local bookstore café. They spend hours working there with the occasional "magazine break," though they make a point not to go on Thursday nights when there's live jazz and too much distraction.

ENHANCE YOUR WORK ENVIRONMENT

Formichelli and Martin are two of the legions of home business owners who fill bookstore cafés and coffee shops each day, working quietly, stopping only for the occasional decaf cappuccino. But there are millions more who would agree with the sentiment expressed by a thirty-year-old son who, when urged by his parents to get out of the house, replies, "Why should I leave home? All my stuff is here."

▪ Design Your Ideal Office

Home decorating magazines and television shows these days are all featuring spectacular new home offices. Many home business owners, like Rob Wilkinson, president of ART on FILE, in Seattle, Washington, have extended their home office environments and enhanced their surroundings. I told you about ART on FILE, a leading producer of images used by colleges and universities worldwide for teaching art history, architecture, and design, in chapter 27. The company's sales are derived predominantly from its Web site, yet Wilkinson has created a spectacular environment in which to live and work that includes a large pond outside the studio, with a miniature village and dam, that has been featured on several Seattle-area garden tours.

■ Add Portable Tools

If working in your home office becomes confining or tedious, you can always move to a more comfortable spot. Rotate the places in which you work by using a notebook computer, personal digital assistant, cordless telephone or cellular telephone, pager with e-mail, or any other equipment that will allow you to work unfettered away from your desk. (What you're reading right now was originally dictated into a microcassette recorder, not the voice recognition software loaded onto my computer. For a change of scene—and to get into the right mood to write about portable technology—I used the small tape recorder so I could work while enjoying the view of the park from beneath the trees here on the rooftop deck above my home office. I wish you could have heard the birds!)

It's easy and inexpensive to add tools that allow you to work anywhere in and around your home. You can use call forwarding to transfer incoming calls from your business line to another line with a cordless telephone that you can carry with you. Or use a line splitter and set up an additional cordless phone to share your primary business line, as described in chapter 23. One home business owner I know, who spends ten hours a day on his telephone arranging film and video production crews and postproduction services worldwide, is as likely to be seen using his cordless telephone by his suburban Maryland pool as he is to be found in his home office.

■ Do Business While Traveling

Most portable office equipment was invented for business-people who must travel extensively away from the office or do much of their work in the field with clients or customers. For example, one Kansas City–based publicist I know travels extensively with a personal digital assistant (PDA), because it's smaller and lighter than a notebook computer yet allows him to carry the extensive list of names and telephone numbers of media contacts he needs to be effective on the road. He can also record activity that takes place while he's away from his home office computer in his PDA, then download it when he returns to the office. So a constant record of important information is continually maintained and updated.

However, as you can see, portable technology is also adaptable to meet the needs of anyone who simply wants to recharge their batteries at the local coffee shop or get a change of scenery. Ruth E. Thaler-Carter, a freelance writer, editor, and publications producer in Baltimore, Maryland, believes the ideal companion on a beach vacation is her notebook computer, which she uses to check e-mail for requests from potential clients. After twenty years as a professional writer, Thaler-Carter knows better than to miss an opportunity. On vacation not long ago in Ocean City, New Jersey, Thaler-Carter checked her e-mail to find two messages from potential clients who responded to her ads. She would have lost the prospects if she hadn't seen the messages until she got back to her home office. Instead, she was able to reply to them promptly, and one resulted in a plum assignment.

Even if taking work along on vacation isn't your idea of freedom, decide exactly what is. For Sue Cross, who someday wants to work full-time from her sailboat, the next wave of technology may make it all possible. Look for tools that give you the freedom to live and work where and how you choose. And if you can't find them today, just wait. The next generation of machines will be along any minute now.

CHECKLIST

✓ Portable tools are essential to home business owners who regularly work in the field or must travel away from their home offices on a regular basis. They're also useful for home business owners who would otherwise spend eight hours or more a day at their desks. Which category applies to you? If your work involves spending long hours in front of the computer or on the telephone, you may be putting your physical health and mental well-being at risk. What can you do to change your routine that may be facilitated by portable technology?

✓ Decide whether you long to be around people and activity, or whether you just want peace and quiet with a different view. If it's people you crave, select portable equipment such as a notebook computer and cellular telephone that will allow you to work from the neighborhood coffee shop or bookstore. If you want peace and quiet and freedom to work anywhere in or around your home, you can also use a notebook computer plus a quality cordless telephone so as not to miss inbound calls from prospects and clients or customers.

✓ What is your ideal work environment? Whether you want to work at the beach or live on a beautiful sailboat, make time today to research the kind of tools that will help you live and work where you choose.

Balance Work and Family

Truth: To be an effective home-based business owner and parent requires family dialogue, support, and setting strong personal boundaries.

■ ■ ■

Home business owners across the country are all concerned with the same issue: how they can balance their family lives while running their own businesses from home. The answer, of course, is complex and there is no single cookie-cutter solution to the myriad challenges your new work- and lifestyle will present. But there are some clear steps you can take to more smoothly integrate work and family, and to involve your children in your business in ways that will help them respect and support you in your work.

FAMILIES AND THE HOME OFFICE

Stephen Rowley, Ph.D., is a psychologist based in Silver Spring, Maryland, whose firm, Rowley Associates, Inc., uses psychological principles to help companies figure out the best ways to support the growth and development of their employees. Rowley and his wife are also the parents of inquisitive five-year-old twin daughters. For the most part, Rowley has succeeded in setting boundaries and making his expectations clear for the twins, but sometimes their curiosity and interest in his work cause some sticky situations.

Rowley's principal client is Microsoft in the United Kingdom, Canada, and the United States. Not long ago, Rowley was in the midst of a conference call with senior Microsoft executives in the United Kingdom. They were deeply involved in a discussion of a training and development program when Corey, one of his five-year-olds, came in and asked if she could speak to the Microsoft executives. When "no" gestures didn't work, Rowley quietly put the phone down to shoo her out the door, then raced back to pick up the receiver. There was silence on the other end of the line. To the Microsoft execs, Rowley had simply disappeared. He hastily "explained" that he just taken a moment to think about what they were saying, and the conversation resumed.

With three full-size computer monitors and two portable computers running in his comfortable home office, Rowley has worked hard to demystify his business and satisfy the twins' curiosity. One thing he's done is to show the girls how to take pages out of his printer and stack them. He says this is particularly useful when a document has forty pages or more. Rowley believes this shows the five-year-olds that his office is place were work is done and also makes them less likely to come in and disrupt his business.

Cindy Rowley, his wife, is a sociologist presently studying interior design. Cindy has her own home office and devotes about 25 percent of her time to doing the company's books and invoices. Steve travels extensively, so he and Cindy sit down for a regular meeting every two weeks to review what's happening in the business and family. Steve says this helps them feel connected—he with the family, and Cindy to the business.

When you own a home-based business, everyone in the family is likely to become involved on some level. John Hoag, an architect based in St. Louis, Missouri, brought his fourteen-year-old daughter, Marina, into the business two years ago to help with filing, typing, and managing databases. Hoag Associates specializes in environmentally friendly architecture, and Marina is becoming increasingly interested in urban planning issues. What originally began as a way of earning summer vacation money has turned into a five-hour-a-week commitment year-round, though it's understood that school activities take precedence. Hoag pays his daughter the same hourly rate he'd pay anyone else and cites scheduling challenges as the only issue, such as when she plans to be with friends and he's counting on her help. Hoag feels Marina is learning some valuable lessons and that working together gives her an appreciation for how small business owners have to juggle to make their businesses efficient and effective. He believes Marina sees and understands that responsibility is a necessity, not an option, and he plans soon to update her work status from an independent contractor to an employee.

▪ Common Myths Versus Reality

There are so many myths about working from home. One of the silliest is that people working from home offices are just there to take care of children. As anyone with a small child will tell you, you can't be the primary caregiver and concentrate on your business. And most home-based business owners don't even try. In fact, an interesting study by the National Foundation for Women Business Owners showed that women who work from home are no more likely to have children under eighteen living there than women who work elsewhere.

However, working from home is a wonderful way to be accessible to your family during the important times. You can schedule around the carpool and be there when your teenagers get home from soccer practice in the afternoons. But it's not a substitute for daycare and you shouldn't expect to be the primary caregiver for small children during your business hours and concentrate on your work at the same time.

The good news is, working from home makes it possible to set up a work schedule that allows you to be available at family times. I know one woman, who was publisher of a magazine for parents, who scheduled most of her workday during the hours her small children were at school and the rest in the evening after they were in bed. And once children get older, many parents, like John Hoag, experience great pleasure from bringing their children into their businesses.

TIPS FOR WORKING WITH FAMILY MEMBERS

■ Have a Family Meeting

It requires ongoing dialogue to make any home office situation work, no matter whether there are children involved or two professionals want to live and work successfully under the same roof. To get off to a smooth start, have a family meeting before you set up your home office. If you're already in business, it's never too late to schedule a meeting with your family, spouse, or roommate to discuss how space in your home will be used. Discuss the times of day the home office space will be off-limits to the rest of the family and what you expect while you're at work. Don't automatically expect family members to make concessions to your business needs. For example, if your teenagers regularly watch television in the family room during the afternoons and you're about to take over their space, you should work together to decide what other part of your home they and their friends can occupy during those hours.

I met a husband-and-wife team of landscape architects while speaking at a conference recently. The husband had worked from home for years and his wife had recently joined him. By carefully planning in advance how their space would be used, they both became happily involved in a project to remodel their home office and set up an area of the exterior of their home to showcase their design skills. Without this level of planning, it's doubtful this couple, or most others who decide to live and work together, could make this transition so smoothly.

▪ Maintain Individual Work Spaces

Linda Gibbon and Dick Bangham are visual artists who work in print, video, multimedia, and performance art. Their company, Rip Bang Pictures of Silver Spring, Maryland, is a multidisciplinary design studio set in a large, two-thousand-square-foot home office that encompasses the entire lower level of their home. Each has a separate workstation and there's a conference area with a fireplace where they can have client meetings. But their office space wasn't always this ideal. Until recently, Gibbon and Bangham spent five years working in the cramped basement of their old home. And Linda describes Dick as laid-back while she's "on hyperdrive" and more organized. Yet their business relationship is relatively free of conflict due to their facility for strong communication and mutual support.

Even if your home office is cramped and crowded, each person must have his or her own space in which to work quietly and uninterrupted. When working with your spouse, sometimes your work styles may conflict. So be prepared to be flexible. When Gibbon and Bangham began working together in what had formerly been his home office, she said they would frequently have discussions about his tendency to accumulate clutter.

▪ Keep Up an Ongoing Dialogue

When you work with your spouse, it's important to have regular meetings to discuss current work and any issues that may arise. Don't wait until there are problems to talk about how things are going. Gibbon and Bangham work at an extremely fast pace—they always have at least half a dozen album covers in some stage of completion and work on a variety of other projects, including television shows and live performances. But they make time several days a week to have meetings over dinner. At the end of a day, they go out to eat and talk about what they have to accomplish. They make lists, review work in progress, and discuss the best way to complete the mountain of work.

■ Define Work Roles Clearly

Each family member who works in the home business should have his or her own areas of individual responsibility. When in doubt, write job descriptions just as you would if you were employed elsewhere. At Rip Bang Pictures, Gibbon handles management and accounting, scheduling, and client contact, as well as some design, while Bangham is principally responsible for production, including video editing and animation. Even with such hectic schedules, the two genuinely enjoy their life and work together. Gibbon says they don't let the little things get to them. They look at the big picture and put small annoyances aside until everyone's calm.

CHECKLIST

✓ Help small children to appreciate your work environment by bringing them into your home office during certain times of the day to participate in special kid-friendly tasks. Let children feel they're helping you and sharing in your work life, and they'll be less likely to be disruptive or resentful of the time you spend alone in your home office.

✓ Agree on how the home office space will be used. Set up a meeting with your roommate, spouse, and any children you have in the household. If you're planning to adapt a space such as a family room for your home office, discuss exactly how the room will be used and at what times of the day it will be out of bounds for the rest of the family.

✓ Establish clearly defined work roles and areas of responsibility for all family members who take part in the home business. They should also have their own individual spaces where they can work without being interrupted.

✓ Keep the lines of communication open with regularly scheduled meetings. Don't wait until there are problems before sitting down to talk.

THIRTY

Achieve Your Ultimate Vision

Truth: Real success comes from making the most of your new lifestyle.

■ ■ ■

When speaking to a large group of home business owners not long ago, I asked them to tell me why they had started their businesses. One fellow raised his hand and said he started his home-based business because he wanted to be there when his teenage sons got home from soccer in the afternoons. When I responded with an additional question, "So are you?" he sheepishly replied, "Not really."

Starting a business is hard work no matter where it's based. Yet after the first initial months, with focused effort, you should be able to adopt a more regular routine that allows you to make the most of your new lifestyle. As your business takes off and you begin to achieve the success you're striving for, you may start to feel overloaded with work, and at times overwhelmed by it. And if you have a family, they will begin to feel the repercussions and may even resent your business and the hours it requires.

DEALING WITH YOUR WORKLOAD

The good news is, you're becoming successful. The bad news is, your business success may stand in the way of achieving your ultimate vision. Throughout this book, you've learned ways to facilitate your new work- and lifestyle. You've been exposed to many options for dealing with overwork—and there are lots of choices.

You can:

- Team with other businesses or individuals.

- Subcontract using independent contractors.

- Hire support staff (don't overlook family members).

- Add technology, such as contact management or desktop publishing software, voicemail for taking orders by telephone when you're unavailable, or portable technology.

- Refer work to colleagues you trust and admire.

- Meet only with qualified prospects.

- Be more discriminating about the work you accept.

- Streamline sales and marketing tactics and adopt those that require less hands-on work, such as by broadcast faxing instead of mailing your newsletter, or by hiring an editor to continually update the content of your Web site.

■ Set a Work Schedule

At least one or more of these options, which are all covered in detail in previous chapters, should help you manage your company's growth while making the most of your new lifestyle. Even so, making the transition to working from home can be challenging. That's why it's important to set a regular schedule and stick to it. It doesn't matter if your work hours are from eleven to seven or the old nine to five. What matters most is that you establish a standard routine.

■ **Get Out and Have Fun!**

Schedule your days to include things you like to do. Isolation can play a detrimental role in your home business success, so it's important to schedule time to get away, even if it's just to take a walk or have lunch with friends. Deborah Dennis, president of Black Rhino Design, an Oakland, California, Web design company, starts her day by working out at the gym, running with her dog, or swimming. She also likes to get out of her home office and into her garden every few hours.

Do you schedule everything except time for fun and relaxation? This is definitely a problem if you tend to work on weekends too. Make a point to schedule one special activity that you enjoy at least once a week. Dennis schedules the occasional workday to begin at six A.M. so she can go to the beach in the afternoon. She finds it rewarding to be in charge of her own time, though she believes it takes discipline.

■ **Stay Focused**

Some people who begin working at home for the first time find they succumb easily to distractions. Do you find yourself doing laundry or washing dishes in the middle of the afternoon when you know you should be working? If household chores nag at you during business hours, you have two basic choices. You can complete all of your chores and get them out of the way before you start work. Or you can make up your mind to go into your office at a specific time and come out at designated hours, such as from noon to one o'clock for lunch. This is a particularly helpful strategy if you find it hard to stay away from the refrigerator during the workday. Take everything you'll need into your office at the start of the business day—a thermos with a beverage, fruit, or other snacks—and work there according to a predetermined schedule.

- ## Set Boundaries with Friends and Family

Should friends, neighbors, or family members try to distract you or interrupt your work, make it clear at what hours you'll be available. I've heard stories from business owners everywhere who say that once they began working from home, friends and neighbors assumed they'd be available to accept packages on their behalf, babysit for their children, and even run errands. It's up to you to state firmly that you're working, and during what hours you can and cannot be disturbed.

- ## Jump-Start Your Mornings

New home business owners often encounter another problem—difficulty getting started at the beginning of the workday. If you're having trouble getting going in the mornings, choose a starting ritual. One fellow was having difficulty adjusting to working from home after twenty-five years in an office a half hour away; he couldn't get his day started. Then he got in the habit of dressing for work, going out to his car, and driving around the block, before parking back in his driveway to begin his workday.

There are a lot simpler starting rituals! For many, having that last cup of coffee signals the beginning of the workday. Starting rituals take on real importance when your morning "commute" is a ten-foot walk from your kitchen table to your living room desk. In that case, a helpful ritual can be as simple as turning off the morning TV show and switching on the radio with quiet background music to signal the start of the workday.

- ## Learn When to Call It a Day

Creating your own business can be an all-consuming, passionate experience. With your office in your home, it's easy to lose track of time. Some people find themselves working at all hours, whenever the mood strikes them. When their office phone rings at ten o'clock at night, they rush in to answer it. If you're having difficulty stopping at the end of the day, choose an ending ritual. One good end-of-day ritual is to select a time to stop work and pick a regular activity, such as checking your e-mail, that signals the close of every business day.

Remember Stephen Rowley from the last chapter, the psychologist who provides behavioral solutions for businesses? He uses the last half hour of his workday to decompress, the same way he would use the time to transition from an office away from home. Rowley checks e-mail, updates his schedule, and uses the last half hour as a time for winding down versus winding up. That way he's better prepared to spend quality time with his wife and twin daughters at the end of his day.

By choosing to work from home, you've made a wonderful, life-enhancing decision. You've chosen to do the kind of work you enjoy in the comfort and warmth of your own home. In these thirty chapters, you've seen a lot of the myths and fallacies surrounding working from home neatly exposed. You've discovered the traps and pitfalls of starting and running a business at home—and learned the truths that will save you from them. Keep up the good work!

CHECKLIST

✓ Set a regular schedule and stick to it. Remember also to schedule at least one special activity a week that you enjoy.

✓ To avoid being distracted by chores or rummaging through the refrigerator during the workday, take everything you need into your home office or to your desk in the morning. Then schedule the times at which you'll leave and return to your office during the day.

✓ Choose starting and ending rituals that help you begin work and make a smooth transition from your desk to your home life at the end of the day.

✓ Adopt strategies that allow you to grow your business while maintaining your quality of life. Review the ideas presented in this chapter and throughout the book, and pick the ones that are right for your business.

INDEX

Page numbers in bold indicate tables.

INDEX

Kim T. Gordon is one of the country's foremost experts on home business success. She is a nationally recognized speaker, magazine columnist, and the author of *Growing Your Home-Based Business*. Gordon consults with Fortune 100 companies. Through nationwide seminars, she has helped thousands of small and home-based business owners achieve their goals. Interviews with Gordon have been featured on television, radio, and in print including CNN, *ABC News with Peter Jennings*, The Wall Street Journal Radio Network, and *Newsweek* magazine. She is president of National Marketing Federation, Inc., a multidisciplinary group focused on small office/home office success. For more information, visit Small Business Now.com (www.smallbusinessnow.com) or call 800-2 SOLVE IT. Gordon lives in Maryland.